UNDER THE RAINBOW CROSSING

By
RUTH ANN FRIEND

Based on a true story

Printed in the United States of America

I

Under the Rainbow Crossing

"The Haunting of a Heartland Home and the Spiritual
Journey That Followed…"

Based on a True Story

By
Ruth Ann Friend

Copyright © 2013 by Ruth Ann Friend

Library of Congress registration #1-973524151

Revised edition 2014

Copyright © 1995, 2003 by Ann Hart

The first edition

ISBN: 978-0-9898255-1-1 (Soft Cover)
ISBN: 978-0-9898255-0-4 (e-book)

Friend Publishing

Ruth Ann Friend
My web site
www.UniversalConversations.com

DEDICATIONS

This book has been written and dedicated to those who still mourn their loved ones and proves the survival of our death.

I would like to thank my loving family for respecting the time I needed to write this book. I dedicate my thanks to all of them and my special friend and teacher Beverly who without her direction and guidance I would still be searching. I consider her as one of my earthly angels.

I thank all of my Spiritual teachers, guides, and guardian angels on the other side and on this one, who have guided me on my path. To those who send Christ' healing and who are holy and from the light.

With a very special thank you to my son David, who I know too be an ancient old soul coming here as my son and spiritual teacher. He helped to open my eyes to the other side long ago, before I began my learning journey. It was he who planted the spiritual insight to me, which was needed for my new beginning.

And last, but never least, to the Holy Spiritual Beings that are connected to us with their great love, lessons, and humor. They have proved that the spirit world can indeed guide us in the most positive way. They have proven without a doubt that there is life after life. Our spiritual family has said, "There is really nothing to fear but fear itself, a man-made illusion."

IV

Foreword

It was August 1993, when I met the most amazing speaker, a man 70 years old. At 36 years old he had died for thirty minutes in surgery on the operating table. The first thing he remembers seeing is a man in a brownish colored robe who spoke to him, "Are you ready to go now?"

"No!" The man was confused and didn't know what was going on!

"What would you like to do?" replied the robed man.

"Go fishing." Instantly he found himself on the bank of a river where he caught six fish and took them home to his wife who was washing dishes. As he talked she didn't seem to notice him or hear him. He sat the fish on the counter and she put her pan on top of the fish! It was then he realized two things could not occupy the same space at once that he must be dead! Everything faded away and there again was the man in the robe.

"Are you ready to go forward now?"

"No!" replied the man, he was afraid.

"What would you like to do now?" The robed man asked.

"Go to the beach." Instantly he was there swimming and enjoying the sunshine until he tired of it.

"Are you ready to go now?" the robed man asked him once more.

"Yes," he said, he didn't know what else to do.

He was then taken to the Holy lands to where Jesus and the two thieves were on the cross. He now wore a brown robe and was told his name was Joseph from the Bible. He was shown all of his lives and beyond past now, all of his wives and children.

Then the man in the brown robe who was his spiritual guide told him, "They were sending him back for he had much work to do on Earth. As it was only an *illusion* and we are there to learn from Earth's experiences and we have all done this before and are looking back at it all. That God is within every one of us. That it's the love you give out to others, to love one another."

By this time 30 minutes had went by and he had been taken to the morgue, washed, shaved, and disinfected with alcohol for the next a.m. autopsy. Just as the attendant put his hands on the drawer that he was placed into he returned to his body. The first thing he noticed was that his body and feet were ice cold and something was over his face! As he pulled the sheet back that he was covered with his eyes opened and for some unknown reason he winked at the attendant! He remembered the poor attendant screaming as he ran for the door! He knew everything that had happened in that moment.

This man was sent back to tell his story over the world and he would be a spiritual teacher for the rest of his life. He would help people throughout his life with his teachings and sharing his remarkable story.

I will never forget meeting this wonderful enlightened man. The day he spoke of his story in the church I saw bright golden light which surrounded him! As he explained what had happened to him the gold light around him radiated from him to me, I believe I could actually see his soul shinning!

I thanked him for sharing his story as I was leaving. He took my hand and said, "We will meet again one day."

PREFACE

What if you began to hear muffled voices, music playing, and strange noises, the rattle of dishes and other objects being moved around? Not to mention seeing *unknown* foot prints in the carpet that is not yours? And soon you would become more aware of these frequent happenings through the days and nights. Most mornings and in the day you would experience the strong fragrance of perfume, flowers, smoke, coffee, bacon and eggs, all alone in your home! Not to mention waking up in the middle of the night to the odor of charred wood burning, jumping from your bed thinking your house was on fire to find nothing wrong with great relief!

The most likely thought one may have is *haunted* but that would really not be the case at all in the long run. I would find out much more was going on than I could ever have imagined! These unexplainable happenings are just a very few of the daily never-ending experiences I have lived with for a long time.

What happened above and many other experiences happened and they are certainly not the usual realm of *paranormal* stories one reads about. This is the most *unique* story in every way that you have more than likely ever heard of. This is a rare account of the truth, and I am relaying these experiences onto you the reader.

I have been blessed to see and have Angels and Beings of the Christ Light with the gifts I have been given. These were given to me to live my life in a very unusual way and I didn't know it yet.

My son David came here to this world be one of my *spiritual* teachers and our lives have been more than phenomenal to both of us... Please read on and share my story.

One night I was awakened by a beautiful glowing Angel being who appeared to me with a message. I was completely mesmerized and completely overwhelmed! This is the feeling and words I was left with.

"And when the voices come they will astound you and fill your very heart and soul for you will never doubt what you hear. To try and describe the feelings' I cannot do your life will never be the same. You know without a doubt that you have indeed been given a special message from a Divine source from another dimension. Such a fine line separates our life here and as we say the other side. The Angels words to me were crystal clear even though the full meaning for me may not be clear at this time. It could be a day, a week, or longer, but it will come and make sense at the right time."

On December 12th, 1995 at 4:30amI awoke suddenly to see my bedroom bathed in golden light. Over to the right side of my bed I recognized the same beautiful, glowing, angel being who I knew to be a messenger of Christ. The radiant angel's hands were cupped together in front of it preparing to release something. Slowly the angels' hands opened and a golden dove was revealed! It began to flutter and soar throughout the room in all its glory. What a breathtaking sight it was!

The dove began to circle over to me and suddenly my late mother' face appeared for a brief moment then she faded away. I knew instantly that she was a big part of this beautiful arrangement and this was a message for me. As I focused back to the dove, I watched as it flew back into the Angel' waiting hands. It was then I heard these words.

"The golden dove shows' the love and compassion to others. Go my child out into the world and spread what has been given to you, that which is in your heart which is filled with love and peace, and that we are all eternal. Your quest is mighty but so is your strength!

You shall endure all with great ease and perseverance you will not fail, you will win, and learn to love your life' journey. It is written in your destiny and we will never forsake you!"

UNDER THE RAINBOW CROSSING

Under the rainbow crossing on a bright and sunny day
I was standing with two children when one of them saw the
Rays. Both said; "Look, Look, an upside-down rainbow how
can that be?" But there it was in all of its glorious colors in front of us
to see.

There was the answer to my prayer but not with rain or thunder
The sign seemed for our eyes only, a private yet public wonder
And inside the rainbow was an angel so beautiful and bright
With colors that made me happy with joy as I took in
the sight.

I retrieved my camera from the house and captured this sight that only
we could see
The angel, who carried this rainbow from heaven to earth for me We
stood and watched in silence the changing of its hue until its colors had
faded into the skies deep blue

I shall treasure that day always it's locked within my heart
Though time may dim my mundane mind this image will never part. It
is etched in my being, my all, my soul, and stays with me in spirit
forever, so warm and vibrant I can
almost hear it.

By Ruth Ann and John
(In loving memory of John Paxton)
October 1993

IX

TABLE of CONTENTS

INTRODUCTION

The experiences I have written about in this book are based on true and accurate accounts of recent events that actually occurred in my presence, and in my house. Which, I don't quite know how else to put this---is haunted! Yes, it is according to some others. My perspective on the episodes I am about to relate however, may seem different than you would expect. Since people usually tend to associate negative images and emotions with the idea of *ghosts* cohabitating in the same space as normal, solid people. Though the strange goings on in my house at first certainly did scare the "you know what" out of me. Since then, they have opened me to brand new ways of thinking, brand new ways of feeling, to new books, and to new friends. In short, to a fascinating and deeply rewarding spiritual path I never dreamed I would encounter much less pursue. It is my hope that you who are reading this book might also become more acquainted with this path. Perhaps like myself through an unfamiliar or an unexpected brush with similar experiences, or at least in a theoretical way.

That you too, may learn as I did to embrace a bigger picture of life. As a result, I found a larger measure of joy and peace, joy and peace, from *ghosts* and *haunted* houses? It sounds crazy I know, but at this point allow me to address your excellent question with an invitation to read on and well, share in my adventure.

I am an ordinary housewife living in a small southern Illinois town. I have been given some extraordinary qualities and abilities, to help me in my life. I do admit to being extremely sensitive to the feelings of others. I grew up quite shy and backward by nature, but through my spiritual experiences I have developed my clairvoyant and psychic abilities. I have been touched by my Heavenly Father Christ, and that is in fact, a real participant in this earthly framework of time and space.

The events and happenings that have regularly occurred in my home would have frightened off most people quickly! It is of course natural to be afraid of what we can't see or what we can't explain. Most of us have probably been raised with *ghost* stories and *scary* movies which perhaps represent an underlying conditioning of fear. Many of us have experienced to not only be afraid, but to become attached to our fears as well. We so often live in fear because we have been taught to live in fear, and perhaps to in some sordid way actually enjoy being afraid. This small book however chronicles the paranormal episodes in my home. Not from the point of view of fear, but of wonder and excitement. Wonder and excitement at finding me so close for so long, to what is apparently a place of intersection between this side and the other!

We have one son, David, and three daughters, Lynn, Deanne, and Michelle. Thirty years ago when my husband Leon and I were house hunting in southern Illinois we first saw the old house for sale in the evening newspaper. That night we called for an appointment to see it. I recalled, that I could remember the house from my childhood years when my family and I would pass by it. Even then I was drawn to the old house as a child always wondering what it was like inside. The big house stood back from the street, dark, run down and scary looking to me!

When my husband and I viewed the house we were astounded at how much work was needed to make it habitable (for normal, solid people that is.)The seller told us the house dated from the mid 1800' and was either going to have to be restored or torn down. He also told us, "That according to the deed a Captain Daughtery from the Civil War was given this land by the government and that at one time it sat in the middle of a cherry orchard (only a lone cherry tree remains today) and it had also served as a boarding house and a stagecoach-stop."

Anyway, since my husband is quite handy with carpentry, electrical systems, and plumbing, we decided that we couldn't pass up the bargain. We bought the house from a couple that had lived in it a very *short* time. (I often wonder if the reason for their departure and this book are the same.)

The house is comprised downstairs of a front parlor, with a large fireplace and staircase to the upstairs in the front. Next there is a middle parlor, a bath and kitchen with another stairway off of the kitchen leading upstairs to five bedrooms. We were once told the back stairway was for the help. (That would be me from now on.)

The main reason as I have mentioned in writing this book is so that it may be a learning tool for others. The accounts herein are recorded in the way that I myself have learned to view such phenomena--- namely, positively or beneficently. All of my life I was conditioned to think the bad outweighed the good by a large measure. I have discovered for me anyway that beneficial events sometimes happen in strange, unusual, even initially frightful or bad ways.

This perspective has granted me restfulness at times when otherwise fear would have taken hold. The journey of life becomes easier, in other words, when one views the world as not divided into the bad and the good. But in a way that permits both to come together so that what is left is well, merely fascinating, intriguing, and rewarding.

The spiritual beings of light have taught me that and you will soon understand how. I don't always succeed now in not worrying and in not always being afraid but the *ghosts* in my house are a continual reminder that while fear is perhaps necessary at times, one's life does not have to be held hostage to it. I feel I am deeply indebted to them for this lesson as well as the excitement that they have brought into our life.

The accounts set forth in this book are placed in approximate chronological order and I have kept meticulous notes in recent years and the description of the accounts. They are however accurate and true. Though I don't always remember the precise dates of some occurrences, especially those that started early in my awaking to the strange phenomena this book is in addition to proffering itself as a teaching devise presented in the form of a very personal (but now public) diary or journal.

Paranormal activity is not always categorized and presented in an organized fashion. Meaning with all encounters being the same type of phenomenon treated in full measure before moving on to the next sort of unexplained and inexplicable activity. Rather, I am here in merely telling my story from the beginning but certainly not to the end. Additional strangeness usually goes on pretty well everyday in our house. All of which I am carefully documenting with pen, camera, tapes, and video camera in which I hope to be able to offer the next phase of this amazing story in a sequel to this volume.

Finally, I wish to mention my mother and grandfather for the preparation they gave me for the events described in this book. I didn't realize it at the time, but now that I am in a position to think back and remember the many stories mother told me as a child, I know they both were blessed. They each had the kind of special sensitivity and gifts that seems to conduct or perhaps *attract paranormal encounters.*

My mother would tell me stories of *spirits* visiting her sometimes with messages, and tell me of *visions* that she could see. As a child I assumed everyone's mother was able to do this. Since having grown up with the stories and at times experiencing such episodes myself I dismissed them as part of someone else's experience not my own. The experiences are now part of my own life. In thinking back, if only I had paid more attention to my mother's extraordinary gift and my grandfather' stories to help prepare me along my spiritual journey.

This is a room full of spirit energy that I photographed.

CHAPTER ONE
What is going on here?

Not long after we moved into our old house over three decades ago in June of 1964, the children began to have strange and frightening experiences. They were often so *scared* that I was forced to spend many nights awake with them in futile attempts to quite them back to sleep. I had not yet encountered any odd *phenomena* in the house and thus reduced their fitful episodes to whatever they may have watched on television, read in comic books, or had seen at the movies. The children would tell me of hearing footsteps, and seeing *see* through people and hearing voices.

They would often complain that something in their room had been moved while we had been away. Sometimes, our son David would run downstairs an hour or two after bedtime complaining that there were flashes of light in his room. "That something had tried to pull him under his bed!" Upon reassuring him that there were no such things as ghosts, lights flashing and monsters' I would take him back to his room which looked perfectly unattended to me. Many nights I would wake up to find David sleeping under my bed. I just rationalized that his imagination was getting out of hand, and gave thoughts to the possibility of therapy for him but no, what about the rest of the children? Was it mass hysteria? Much later, I would understand how sensitive and open young children are to the paranormal.

The years passed and I spent more time awake than asleep it seemed due to such incidents with the children. At that time I never noticed anything extraordinary. Perhaps I was just too tired or distracted to experience what they were experiencing, or because the house was filled with so much commotion and noise of the children, I don't know for sure. My husband and I would sometimes laugh together about our children's imagination.

I couldn't understand for the life of me why after all of our reassuring the kids could not let go of their nonsense. In any event before I knew it the children had grown up, married and left home. It wasn't long after the last child was reared that I began realizing, much to my *horror* that even though I was alone in the house at night (my husband worked a second shift at the time) I wasn't alone in the house at night! The stories the children had for years told of voices from nowhere and see through people were immerging and objects were moving by themselves! These things were suddenly brought from the shadows of their youthful imagination right into my life! I began doubting my own sanity and contemplating the possibility of therapy for myself! But of course one doesn't discuss, at least not at first, things that go *bump* in the night. Instead, I spent the evenings at my daughters' who lived nearby just to keep her company, at least this is what I would tell her. There was no need to tell her anything as long as I could stay with her until my husband came home from work.

I continued to be on guard in the house whatever the hour of the day or night and wished for a set of eyes in the back of my head. This was especially when the hair rose on the back of my neck and cool breezes whisked by me. Staying at home some nights, I would remain awake for a long time listening to the sound of footsteps coming up the stairs and down the hall then entering our bedroom! I was completely *terrified* and I would break into a cold sweat afraid to breath or move.

At other times I would go to bed early due to some recurring physical problems I was having, only to awaken later to the sounds of muffled voices and sometimes, music. Initially, I assumed that my husband had come home from work and was watching a little television before retiring. Some nights upon hearing talking, I would get up and walk down the staircase to investigate, and the voices would suddenly stop! I would find myself at the bottom of the stairs starring at a pitch black room! It was all quite *eerie* to say the least!

Upon getting use to awakening to voices and music I would attempt to sneak down the stairs on whatever was there, but the commotion would always fade away as I quietly approached. On some occasions, instead of awakening to the voices and music I would be startled by the sounds of loud footsteps and still half- asleep automatically think or perhaps pray that Leon had come home. I would immediately lean-over and turn on the lamp but when the light pushed back the darkness of the bedroom there of course would be no one there! I began to remind myself of how my children must have felt all of these years' growing up when we didn't take them seriously. Now, here I was afraid to come out from under the covers at night! And this wasn't out of some movie!

I will never forget the first object I saw move---saw move mind you, which is quite different from merely noticing that something has been mysteriously displaced though I have experienced plenty of mysteriously displaced and misplaced things as well. It was not at night but during the day, a hot summer day.

I was outside painting the wooden siding on our house and I decided to take a break by going into the house to the bathroom. Upon entering the bathroom I immediately heard the sound of tapping, Tap, tap, tap, slowly at first and then more rapidly. When I looked at the vanity I saw a large full bottle of lotion rocking back and forth under its own power! I was so startled I froze, I was spellbound and I couldn't get out a sound! "How in the world can this be happening?" I mumbled. I watched the bottle rocking motion slowly increase in speed until the bottle was a blur. Finally, it began to gradually slow down until it came to a stop! Upon regaining some of my senses I quickly turned and left the bathroom forgetting why I went into it!

I decided not to tell anyone about the incident for fear that the family would think I had *cracked*. I knew I had not been my usual self for a while, if only they knew. Also, during this period I was at home one evening watching some television and heard a terrible crashing noise from the dining room. I ran to the kitchen from where I had been sitting, to my horror I saw that the light- fixture that hangs over the dining room table had fallen out of the ceiling onto the table! The hand-painted antique glass shade was practically eggshell thin and a favorite of mine. I rushed over to see the damage and I was shocked to see there was not even a chip or tiny crack! There was no way the fixture could have fallen out of the large support beam in the ceiling in the first place and without breaking! But there it was, not only intact, but also standing perfectly upright as though it had been placed by hand on the dining room table! I questioned myself, what in the world is going on?

On September 23, 1987 my father passed away due to an advanced stage of cancer and an attendant case of pneumonia. Five weeks before his death he had to be placed in a nursing facility. This was in order to keep him as free from pain as possible. I had a premonition that he would get pneumonia and cross over and sadly he soon did.

Perhaps, because our family over the years had become particularly sensitive to paranormal experiences or perhaps for some other reason we each had an experience. At the moment my father died, my son, one of my daughters, one of my brothers, and myself, all had strange *encounters* which we are convinced were derived from his passing. My father died in my daughter Lynn's arms in the hospital (to which he had been taken by ambulance) across town from the nursing home. At the moment of his passing she remembers what she describes as a *swooshing* sound that she felt rushing through her. She knew at that moment his spirit had left his body! Somehow she also knew that he was waiting for her to be the one who would release him. Being in a coma for several days my dad had held on until she was with him. She interprets' this rather vivid and memorable moment as resulting from being so close to her grandfather that he had waited for her to make his transition from one kind of life to another.

My son David was living in another state at the time but was very aware that his grandfather's death was imminent. That same evening he was talking to Jim his dear friend at his home. Suddenly both of them looked up toward the ceiling to witness a small, bright sphere of light hovering over them! David and his friend Jim interpreted the light as an indication that grandfather had died. That he was by way of the light, reassuring David that his death and all deaths are not as final as they appear to be.

And that night I personally was lying in bed distraught because I had not reached the hospital in time to be with my dad during his final moments on earth. As I lay there feeling a terrible emptiness, all of a sudden there suddenly appeared a quite beautiful exhibition of LIGHTS above my bed quite like they look on the 4th of July! Yes, I was fully awake and witnessed an exquisite display of laser-like multicolored lights, and while I watched the word *celebration* was given to me by my dad! I then realized that he was letting me know he was just fine! This was a celebration meaning that he was free, out of pain, and in the arms of Christ! Now, regardless of how it happened and why, I took great comfort in my bedroom that night! Dad knew I needed his visit at this particularly traumatic and transitional time in my life. I had found peace that night and slept soundly.

When my daughter Lynn returned from the hospital that night still amazed and perplexed by her *swooshing* experience she was exhausted. She prayed she might be granted another reassuring encounter. When she awoke the next morning she found the window in her room which had been painted tightly shut for years, wide-open, to the outside world! She also discovered the small electric alarm-clock given to her

4

by her grandfather which she kept on a shelf several feet from her bed sitting upright on her pillow!

But perhaps the most shocking experience of all happened to one of my brothers. On that evening he had laid down on his bed and as he was resting there he suddenly saw our father standing at the foot of the bed! My brother was on vacation in Hawaii and he had not yet received word of our father's death and was rather alarmed at the experience! He had never experienced anything that might be classified as paranormal and is quite frankly, the world's greatest cynic on such matters. Upon witnessing our father's spiritual presence in his bedroom the telephone rang with the news of our fathers passing.

Because of all of these simultaneous experiences happening to each of us independently and many miles apart, our family can't help but conclude that in various ways it all happened. Our father and grandfather made the rounds on his way from this life to the next. More importantly, these episodes surrounding the death of my father reinforced within us a strange sort of restfulness intertwined with a peacefulness. It is as though the attention grabbing to say the least, nature of the paranormal at first inclines one toward fear. But after one in effect gets use to them the resultant product that they leave in the wake is a calmness and ease.

The belief system dispensed by some of the churches so often seems to not only acquaint one with fear, but moreover it seems to have the effect of making us permanently afraid. I don't mean to speak overly pejoratively about the institutional church. I am only speaking from my own background, my own roots. The paranormal I have firmly decided, in other words is not necessarily an illusionary and negative reality that stems from psychopathology or the devil. As I have experienced it is a wonderful (if at times abrupt) experience. I was learning I was living a very positive reality that has the capacity and perhaps intention to assist me in getting a view of the big picture. In the big picture and in my own view of it can be very conductive of costiveness when I needed it and I have never been acquainted by anything other than oddly enough, experiencing the paranormal, as when my dad passed away with his spirit visits to us.

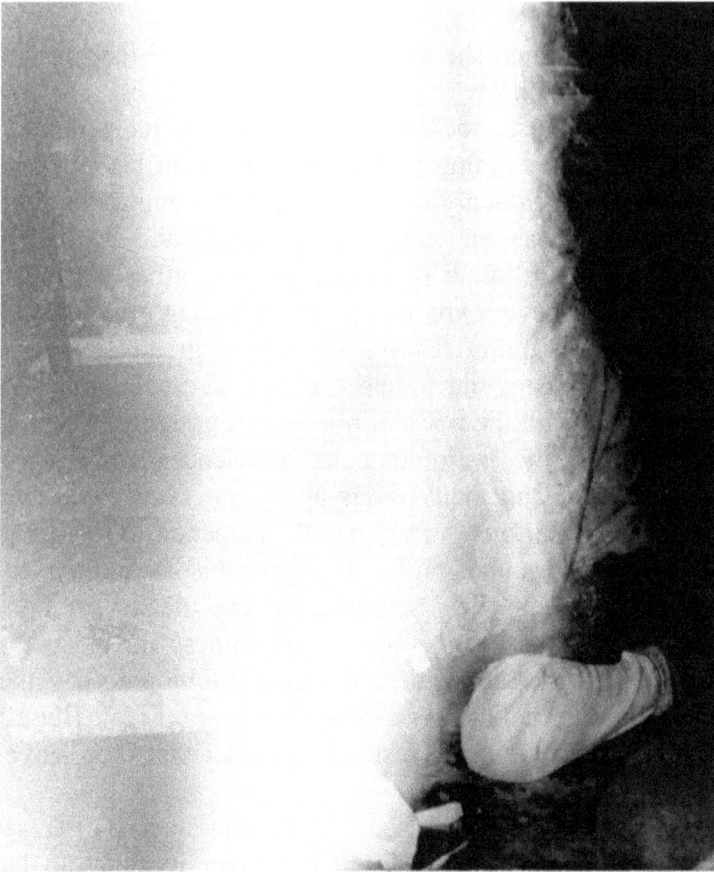

Pictured is my Dad appearing in his spiritual form of golden light (a back view) his shoulders down, taken on Christmas watching us open gifts, and taken without a flash.

At the funeral for my father, my mother was unable to speak or stand without the aid of my brothers at the funeral. I knew her grief was overwhelming and her rare condition was terminal not even allowing her the release of tears. She could not talk, walk, or was able to express grief, and to know what is going on well, she was a prisoner in her own body. Her illness let her keep her mind but slowly destroyed her body eventually leaving her like an infant. I could only think of how she endured her own illness, and watched my father with his cancer and his loss of memory. This was the worse for her when dad didn't know her or anyone else anymore.

We had kept my parents in their home for many years until they needed much more care than we could ever provide. Then my mother also had to endure the pain of knowing she and dad were being taken from their home to never see it again. My heart broke; this was one of the most heartbreaking times in my life.

After the funeral she was taken by ambulance back to the nursing home. I stayed with her that evening and the next few days. She not only couldn't not speak but could not hold a pen to write for years. But her thoughts came to me to give her a piece of paper and a pen. The thought seemed very odd indeed because it had been years since she had actually been able to use her hands. Still, for some reason I followed my intuition and to my surprise she did her best to take the pen. We mostly used telepathy to read each other's mind meaning to talk with our thoughts. I folded her fingers around the pen and with great labor she wrote these words "Daddy was here!" Then she looked towards the other side of the room where her gaze stayed most of the time. I knew she was seeing my dad! I remembered the gifts she had with seeing into the spiritual world growing up. I have kept the paper she wrote on that day in my Bible and I shall treasure it always.

Since that day I have seen my dad with his visits to me many times. The next time I saw dad in spirit was shortly after his celebration night as he passed over. Later on, he appeared to me in what you may call a dream state but it was a vision; he looked so healthy and young with a radiant smile upon his face. He called out to me to let me know he was happy and not to worry, he was just fine! I would continue to receive many of his messages preparing me in my life for many things to come.

After that peculiar time I saw dad I drove immediately to the nursing home. As soon as I got to mother's room I closed the door and said, "I can see dad too!" The look on her face was priceless! At last, she was comforted with the knowledge that someone else in the family could see what she had always been able to see. I don't know the precise manner in which my mother perceived father appearing before her, but his image varied when he appeared to me. At times he seemed very normal manifesting himself in the usual clothing he wore in his lifetime. Other times, he seemed to be made more of golden light. Sometimes he was surrounded by other spiritual beings comprised of the same translucent and glowing hue. Needless to say such things never frighten me I feel a rush of complete love and peace whenever he appears. After all, who am I that I should be so blessed to such experiences as this? Why would anyone be afraid of a loved one in spirit that only loves you and has come to give you peace?

I must confess some pleasure at saying that, the paranormal episodes in our peculiar house have not left my husband the skeptic untouched!

This is a female spirit forming in front of the bathroom mirror.
Look closely and you will see a Buddha through the form,
which I do not have.

One of his first experiences was in the fall when he was working upstairs. He was working in a closet and of course had the light turned on. Every time he left the closet to get something he needed when he came back the light would be turned off! I happened by the room in which he was working at a moment when he had just returned from a break. He was busy muttering to himself "I know I left this light on!"

I told him some of the episodes that have crossed my path, but he would always chuckle ever the skeptic. Then in April, he became a real believer yet still reluctant to admit it!

I awoke early on that morning in April and I lay there warm and snug listening to the small alarm clock making tick-tock noise. I remember thinking how unusually loud the clock was. Since it was not quite time to get up I let the sound lull me back into a semi-conscious state. All of a sudden, I heard an extremely loud crash and the sound of the alarm from across the room! I shot up and saw what I thought couldn't be happening! The alarm clock was not three feet away from me by my bedside but across the room and sounding its alarm! I felt my heart trying to leap out of my chest with the feeling of complete and utter fear! I could tell that a cold sweat was beginning to bead on my skin. Leon was groggy, but I managed to shake him awake. He looked across the room at where the alarm clock now lay. "You're' never going to believe this, but our alarm clock just flew off the table by itself and crashed beside our dresser!" He looked shocked "Well, how in the world did that happen?" I was wondering the same thing! I had been too far away from it to have accidentally knocked it off from my bedside, and even if I had been close enough I could certainly not hurl it across the room! This sure got both of our attention!

Since that time I have concluded that whatever the specific reason for such events they are nevertheless indicative of someone or something trying to get our attention. The most rational response is to become terrified as Leon was on that April morning. So far, we had never been injured or harmed in any way. It's funny; I can't help but think that there is an unknown consciousness or perhaps several from somewhere besides here, directing these things causing these episodes of spontaneous movement. Quite obviously some slight damage is sometimes done as with our light-fixture and alarm clock nevertheless, there has never in my experience been any physical harm done in the proximity of the moving objects. So now I try and think more clearly of the cause in the face of such strangeness. For some reason I feel blessed to be witness to the events. I believe I am learning by these entities wanting to gain my attention in this way. They continue to give me a sense of being in school and that I am learning of another world! I can't imagine this coming from anything other than the paranormal experiences I have encountered and this is what my intuition tells me.

As time passed I gradually became more and more curious. I began to wonder if I would actually feel the touch of a ghost and I use the term ghost rather loosely. Since I don't know exactly what or who resides in our home other than what I know of. I do believe them to be conscious Beings of some order and since ghost is a brief and familiar word. I do feel uneasy using this word anymore because I feel there is much more going on here than a type of ghost. Who knows, but I must have sensed what was about to occur because it wasn't long before the immaterial became palpable.

The first time I was actually contacted was after I had gone to bed as I was lying there trying to go to sleep all of a sudden I felt something touch my left shoulder and soon I felt several light pats! I lay completely still almost afraid to breath. Though Leon was already asleep right next to me I couldn't get my hand to move from under the covers to awaken him. I surrendered to my paralysis by thinking that if I had been able to awaken him there wasn't anything he would be able to do anyway.

Even though he was beginning to know that something strange seemed to be residing in the house with us I hadn't told him about most of the paranormal episodes and I didn't know how much support he would be able to offer me and really what could he do? I lay there a short while until this presence stopped its contact with me. I strongly felt this was a comforting presence almost as if saying, everything will be alright. I would later find my feeling was right! I had felt a caring affection as if this entity was some kind of a loved one! There was so much going on I was undecided.

A few nights later we decided to go shopping to get away for awhile. Upon our return in the bathroom we discovered several articles unexpectedly scattered about on the floor: a can of air-freshener, hair spray, a bottle of lotion, and other toiletries. We just looked at each other knowing that the items had been in their proper places when we left. We didn't discuss the incident, picked up the articles then retired to the sitting room to watch television. We were at a loss.

A couple of nights later we both awakened to a loud crash! The noise awakened Leon this time which means it sounded like a bomb exploding! For some reason when we went to the adjoining room from where the noise came from nothing was upset or out of place. Yes, it was getting a little more difficult to sleep around here. I am without a doubt there is no time in our spirits invisible world.

I began to wish I had an experienced spiritual adviser of some sort to talk to about these events. I also began to wonder if we should sell the house and move to some place normal. But what of the unsuspecting buyer, could we lie to him or her? I knew we wouldn't. Besides, even though I had been terrified many times by the strangeness I was becoming less intensely so in recent months. I was even beginning to entertain the notion that I was becoming somewhat obsessed with wanting to learn more about the bizarre encounters and with the loving conscious entities that certainly seemed to be directing them. To experience a visit from my father was one thing, but all of the other episodes were something else. I had so much to think about and I began sharing with my son David who was in the Air Force and was also a gifted clairvoyant. He had had many things happen to him from a child on. We use to talk of these things when he was home.

Summer came and we decided to go on vacation. We wanted to get away for a while and perhaps get a perspective on our situation at home. Our youngest daughter agreed to house sit for us. It was her house-sitting that summer that made her decide something, that she would never come into our house alone ever again unless she just had to! She would check the house each day take in the mail and do her laundry, simple enough. But while folding her clothes one day she began to hear a loud static noise coming from the front parlor. Fear began to run through her after all, she had been raised in this house and could remember the strange happenings. Slowly she made her way to the big double doors that were closed to the parlor waited for a moment then mustered all of her courage and swung the doors open! First thing she saw was my father's old television set on and running with a snowy screen! The volume had been turned-up high even though the ON/OFF switch was turned off! The old television had been temporarily stored there and had never been used. She managed to find the remote control but none of the buttons would affect the television! She tried the buttons directly on the television but nothing would turn it off! She

11

then thought to pull the plug from the wall-socket and it turned off at last! She flew out of the house with few steps.

When we arrived home a few days later she came out to the car before we even opened the doors. She was babbling so fast we had to slow her down. We left our luggage in the car for a moment after she told her experience to us. We quickly went into the parlor and upon experimenting with the television found it to be in perfect working order! To this day I doubt she would want to spend a moment by herself in this house. This event had had a big effect on her.

Speaking of electrical malfunctions around this time and I am speaking of the late 1990's now, strange phenomena related to electricity were beginning to manifest themselves right before my eyes! At that time the phenomena was oriented mostly with the telephone and in the kitchen.

I had been very ill and my daughter Lynn had tried unsuccessfully to reach me by telephone. She knew I was there and too sick to leave anywhere. She would repeatedly call me but upon connecting to my telephone would never receive an answer. She began to imagine all sorts of things in her mind. On that day I was home in bed sick and unfortunately the telephone did not ring at my end. Another of my daughters also tried to telephone me through my illness but would invariably get a busy-signal even though I was still not able to be on the telephone. The only exception to the busy-signal was when someone supposedly at my end picked up the phone. No one said a word when my daughter kept saying "Hello, Hello?"

Upon experiencing another mysterious and frightening event she finally decided to come over to the house. She thought I was perhaps still too ill to respond to her telephone call, or that something worse had happened. She had to muster her courage in order to do this because the memory of the autocratic television was still vivid in her mind. As she entered the house and my bedroom she found the phone on the floor beside my bed! I was not home!

My friend had taken me to the doctor's office earlier that day and I had not returned home yet. My daughter had finally gotten through to "no one!" That episode only reinforced her reluctance to enter the house alone again. When I arrived I took pictures of the phone on the floor; later in the photos bright orange and gold light was all around the bed, phone, and across my pillows! As it has turned out and since that time other people have reported to me the exact same phenomenon with the phone. That is they have placed at times a call and made a connection, only to speak into an unresponsive silence at my end. At other times a connection was made and a MALE voice answered the phone with no one at home! It was also not uncommon to hear a little girl's voice too! The spirits seem to prefer to dabble with electrical devises and this pattern has certainly been the case in our house. Remember, spirits are energy and use energy in the way they want and need to. This is simple for them to do…Everything is energy.

Similarly, on June 10th, Fathers Day, I was inside the house and had a fan on me as I worked. All of a sudden I heard the ON/OFF button on the fan sound its click and the fan turned off by itself. It would stop each time I turned it back on and finally it stayed. By the way June 10th was also my mother and dad's wedding anniversary. I couldn't help wondering if they were here trying to gain my attention. I was finding out more all the time that some of the strange occurrences' related to important dates. In addition, at certain times lights would flicker on and off while the lights beside them on the same fixture would remain on. At other times when talking on the telephone another phone in the house would start ringing as if I had hung up, we only have one line!

During that summer our microwave refused to operate, the timer would not shut off. Everything I tried the microwave would not work so I finally pulled the plug. We took it the repair shop only to have the technicians' call back saying they could not find a thing wrong with it and we could pick it up from then on it worked perfectly.

Our washer and dryer also broke that summer then mysteriously fixed themselves before the repairman even started to work on them. Then our window air conditioning unit we have downstairs began to stop abruptly for no reason. We checked all the connections but called a repairman anyway even though the air conditioner had been in perfect working order. Before the repairman could do anything I got an idea. I decided to act as though the cause of the malfunction was conscious, reasoning, and reasonable. I mentally explained to this consciousness because of how hot it is to us normal solid beings we really needed to have the air-conditioner functioning. Then don't ask me how or why the unit popped back on by its self! I recall the repairman charging for his time but scratching his head at the same time. I was beginning to learn that the other side could hear me! I was elated, but Leon was in a state of well, shock! I had been learning that I could definitely communicate with this energy.

It was fall again when I began to experience more encounters in my dreams. I was beginning to feel like I was in school being given lessons but not too close together. I was given enough time in between to absorb them. I was right on track even though I did not know it then. My firm belief is that we do receive visits from departed individuals during sleep states; and other times. We think these are only dreams, but I believe much more is going on than we can during conscious moments imagine.

On the night of October 2nd, 1998 that my father came to see me again while I was having a vision. I opened my eyes and looking up and there he was! I had felt his presence. He was walking towards me with his arms outstretched as though he was going to hug me and I simply can't describe the feeling in my heart. It had been a long time now and I remembered crying out "Oh, dad but your dead!" He was crying for joy and I in turn was too and so very grateful to see him! What is more I could read his thoughts. He called me by his nickname for me and my heart swelled with love. As we embraced each other I laid my head on his chest and I could *actually* hear his heartbeat! I thought "how can this be?" But it was as real as in his life! Dad looked so young and in his prime, full of health and he was dressed in his usual clothing he wore each day in life.

When he died he was only a thin shell of himself. I had asked him to come to me many times since the last visit and I had a feeling for some reason he did try to get through. For reasons unknown to me he was not able to appear to me again until now. Maybe he did come to me and I just was somehow not aware of him? This encounter was only another of many. I believe with all my heart that he returns to assure me that there is "life after life" and that our spirits do live forever. Yes, there were wonderful positive forces at work around me.

I was convinced that it was not my own meager, if sensitive nature that was conducting these encounters, but the *haunted* house also was playing a central role in facilitating these strange events.

I began to want to seek out a teacher, a guide, someone who was actually experienced in such manners. But where was such an individual especially in the middle of the rural heartland, the Bible belt? And if I openly advertised for such an individual I was sure to be labeled a nut, a witch, or something worse.

In the spring I began to feel even more urgency about finding someone who could help explain the paranormal to me. I wanted to know that I wasn't alone in the world in this regard. For some unknown reason one morning I got into my car and just started driving not knowing where I was heading or why. This had to be the doorway opening for me. I drove to a neighboring town about twenty-five miles away and pulled up in front of a shop I had never seen before. Little did I know I was being guided. The shop seemed to carry everything from antiques to wallpaper. I walked in and began gazing at a wallpaper sample when a woman asked if she could help me? I couldn't believe the words that popped out of my mouth: "I'm looking for just the right paper for my house it's haunted, it's a haunted house." Why in the world did I say that? I didn't tell anyone about my house! I had been extremely careful to never speak about it and especially to strangers about my paranormal experiences. I would soon find out why I said what I did. I was being led to the person I needed without knowing it.

To my surprise she immediately sat down saying, "that she too was very interested in such matters and if I would tell her something of my house she would be most grateful." I told her I was hesitant to say anymore because of how I wished the house, for the sake of privacy to remain anonymous. But I did relate a little, enough to encourage the woman to tell me she had a friend who could help me. She was a psychic and clairvoyant named Beverly who she knew could help me. Then the woman gave me Beverly's telephone number.

As I look back now, it is comforting to succumb to the temptation to believe that everything in our lives is filled with purpose whether or not we realize it at the time. Such certainly seems to be the case with my unexpected volunteering of information about my house to the woman in the unfamiliar shop.

It was a few weeks however before I made the call. Perhaps I was still afraid of going public. What finally made me make this pivotal call began early one morning as I lay in bed getting ready to get up. My right arm was stretched out upon the next pillow my husband had left for work so I had the luxury of the entire bed. All of a sudden I felt a little child's hand stroking mine! I knew somehow this was a little girl spirit. She was so full of warmth and love she melted my heart. I couldn't see her but I had no doubt that a little girl was present. I was completely overwhelmed by the feeling her touch gave me. It was very much like the radiant emotion that parents have for their children when they are born. I began to think of making the call.

Later on, sometimes at night she would climb upon the bed staying on my side and move the sheets around. I figured she was playing and getting my attention at the same time. Sometimes she would touch my face in a loving gentle way. At other times it felt as though she were tickling my feet as any child might do.

After my experience a few weeks after my honesty at the shop I decided my aloneness in these matters had gone on long enough I made the call to Beverly. I just had to have some help on these matters.

The date was February 28, 1995. While I dialed the number to this psychic woman I thought of how I would begin. I need not have worried because when she answered the phone she said, "I'm so glad you called; I have been waiting to hear from you and not to tell her anything that she would tell me." I sat there in amazement as she described our home, the rooms, staircases, and the many spiritual encounters. She could sense what we had experienced in the house. She knew things no one else could have known, things I had not shared with anyone! The hair stood up on the back of my neck as she explained what had given rise to so much activity in our house. It was the rehabilitation and remodeling that we had been doing to it. One of the ghosts or spirits she said, "Didn't want any changes made that he wanted the house to remain as it had for the past decades. He had been a runaway slave in the mid-1800' and was originally from Mississippi. He had performed odd jobs and some carpentry work at our house in order to earn his keep and he slept in the old shed on the dirt floor next to the kitchen. Our constant hammering during remodeling must have really annoyed him!"

She told me of a female presence, a woman called Queenie possibly in charge of the household at some time. She also sensed a lumberjack, very tall and in his 30's when he died (probably the same one the children use to wake up and see and tell me about.)

The little girl whose touch prompted me to make this call was named Katie Jane and had died at five years old.

"There were others too, at least eight," she said. Beverly related what appeared to be going on in our house with objects moving by themselves, electrical abnormalities, and audible voices from no visible source were intangible, yet palpable spiritual presence, and also the visible spiritual phenomenon was an effort to communicate.

16

Can you imagine she said, "what it would be like if you were in another time and space, or outside of them where words bend and break and you wanted not only your presence to be known but to communicate besides? Movement, noise, electrical disturbances seem to be common techniques not to frighten but to communicate" She then told me she sometimes worked on or investigated such matters with a friend and asked if we could set up an appointment to tour my house. Her voice was so full of love and understanding I could hardly wait!

A week later the big day finally arrived; it was the end of the first week in March. I went to get last-minute refreshments before they would be knocking on my door. When I pulled into the driveway I noticed the front door was wide open. Were they here already? Did they arrive before I could get back? Where was their car? I walked in carrying a sack of groceries to find Leon still working in the kitchen. He had no idea the door had been opened! I had left by the back door so I knew I hadn't left the front door open. I figured the ghosts knew company was coming and the trick with the door was their way of welcoming Beverly and her friend, Christopher.

Soon they arrived and I greeted them at the already open door. When they entered I noticed Beverly looking at something I couldn't see. I didn't ask any questions at that point; I just welcomed them warmly and asked them to do whatever they normally did in cases like this. Chris was extremely well humored which put me at ease so Leon and I followed along behind them as they began the tour.

I was anxious to know what Beverly would do when she walked into the hall where I often smelled smoke and wood burning. The smell always seemed related to my sensing of little Katie.

As Beverly went up the back stairs and stepped into the back hall she stopped and said, "Oh Chris do you smell it?" She quickly backed out of the hall clutching her stomach and apologizing, saying "that something in the air was making her sick." After she collected herself she said, "It was not the smoky smell that had caused her pain, but the images that had raced into her mind she had *picked up* a scene of the reason for Katie's early tragic death."

I don't know exactly what images Beverly saw but my heart broke for the small child who had been treated brutally! I told Beverly that Katie and I seem to have a strong bond between us and perhaps I felt this way because we had known each other before in another lifetime?

As Beverly began to feel better we continued on. Chris, who is also an ordained minister, was making friends with as he said, "the rooms and their usually invisible occupants." He was attempting to give permission for the spirits to move toward the light. That is if they wanted to be released and if that was where they wanted to go. We entered the bedroom by the hall as Beverly explained "that both areas, the hallway and our bedroom, were the heart of our home." Meaning these areas was extremely busy with activity of one kind or another and not only at night when the movement of us normal, solid people was at its lowest level.

Beverly told us how the refined older woman spirit would walk by the bed at night. She would stop and rest her left hand on the bed post, and gaze at us while we slept. Our room was so busy she explained! I thought, how true. Chris sat down in an old antique chair and said, "Uh-oh, I think I'm sitting in someone's chair!" Beverly laughed and informed us that was where the older lady likes to sit. The elegant older lady loved to sit in that chair meaning no harm to anyone.

We talked about the front door being open before they arrived and Beverly told us that one of the female spirits had welcomed both of them into the house. She picked up that years ago the spirits received very little company and that they were still enthralled by visitors. Since that time I have been able to sense the same thing: You can, I think, feel their excitement at such times. There have also been some visitors who the spirits did not want here! They would be of a negative nature and the house would suddenly become very cold, sometimes cold enough to see ones breath in the air! Those few never came back.

In our family room is a beautiful antique library table that we had purchased and soon Beverly walked over to it I could tell she was picking up on it. She put her hands on it asking, "Where did you get this beautiful table?" Without waiting for a response she then said, "it had belonged to a young schoolteacher and that she sort of came with the table!" Apparently spirits can be attached to not only certain places but to possessions they loved in life as well. They often stay with their possessions after death. It makes sense to me since the table would have been where the teacher graded her papers and enjoyed the work she loved.

We finally walked through the entire house and then sat down to discuss things. First Beverly assured us that all the presences were positive in nature, harmless in other words. Although the runaway slave from Mississippi, did stay rather annoyed with the constant remodeling being done by my husband in the kitchen. Since we had not known of any presence in the kitchen before perhaps the runaway was dormant. Then the remodeling began with hammering and tearing out the ceiling, which, so close to his area caused him to sort of awaken and stir. I could put myself in his place and sort of understood how he must have felt. I remember when Chris looked into our kitchen for the first time and saw the mess, he said, "My God, no wonder he's upset!" The kitchen looked rather as if an explosion had occurred! Chris once again blessed the house before they left that day.

I felt good knowing so much more than before my two new friends arrived. What a relief I felt now, but I'm not sure how Leon felt about staying here. I like to think that the ghosts' or spirits' were aware of their choice now: whether to go or stay.

Beverly had spoken of how much the little girl named Katie loved me and wished to stay close to me. I felt the same way actually; she's become sort of like one of my own family. She feels like some kind of relation, a type of daughter, another sister, to my daughters and son. She is like family; no matter how odd this may sound to you the readers. Beverly next looked at our children's pictures and told me about them without having been apprised of the situation. She began talking about the medical problems my oldest daughter was experiencing. "Tell her to see a doctor as soon as possible because she has an imbalance and needs hormone therapy."

I told my daughter later, who followed the advice and she was in fact shortly thereafter diagnosed with an imbalance and placed on hormones. Finally, we knew the reason for her distress while growing up.

Beverly was still looking at the photographs of our children, then explained that Deanne our second oldest was an old soul and very quiet. She always stayed in the background never making waves, again Beverly was exactly correct.

Next she spoke of David, our son. "He was very psychic, and also a very old soul and that he would become a healer and she felt a particular connection with David and that in all probability she and David had been friends in another lifetime. That he was very sensitive with much compassion for everyone and everything and that he had suffered allot from the brutality and malevolence of people."

Chris spoke of our youngest daughter Michelle, "that she is a comedian, very witty, full of energy and speaks her mind very quickly," he said. All of this was true as well. Beverly then turned to me and asked "if she could take my hand?" She explained to me "that she could feel the love and light coming from my heart and that it flowed into hers." I was speechless: I had never heard such a beautiful thing said to me.

Like so many people who have been conditioned while growing up with other children I thought little of myself. I had never achieved self-confidence. Beverly said, "That I would begin to increasingly know and love myself from that moment." Still grasping my hand she then spoke of my husband, "a good soul, a hard worker, a treasure to his family and friends." Correct again.

That evening there was a tremendous amount of activity in the house. The spirits were especially active on that night. I wondered if they were excited and discussing, perhaps even processing, the visit from Beverly and Chris. I sure was glad to learn from Beverly that everything checked out positive and harmless. Armed with this new knowledge (or at least intuition) I decided that I was going to have another longer conversation with the runaway slave. I wanted to tell him that if we had not purchased the house and begun restoration he would probably be looking for a new place to live in!

Despite the history of this house and my family's exposure to it I wanted to have this conversation alone. I guess I still felt uncomfortable about appearing to be talking to an empty room. I had named the slave Joseph and when I later mentioned this to Beverly she asked, "Why I had chosen Joseph?" I told her I just felt this was his name. She paused for a moment checking her "screen" as she calls it, apparently a mental chalkboard of sorts on which messages are given to her and to my surprise she said, " Joseph was in fact his name!"

I must admit that when I attempted the conversation Joseph did not audibly respond, but I certainly felt as though he had heard me and appreciated my attempt. Since then we have had no more problems. Now whenever I leave the house I call to Joseph to watch over things while we are away. I firmly believe that if a burglar were to attempt a break in, Joseph and perhaps the rest of the spirits would do something to dissuade him or her. Who knows, since no one has tried to burglarize the house that I know of? But I can't help but think that perhaps we have the finest security system money can't buy!

I also feel that our lumberjack spirit is also a special guardian of the premises. I have seen him many times now as he appeared in his earthly life. He looks to be in his thirties, dark hair, mustache and beard, kindly, very tall, and quite handsome. He seems so lonely however; I have gotten that he is waiting for someone to return to him, a lost love. He is seen mostly in the west bedroom by the window most of the time or downstairs.

Beverly has said, "That for some reason this house seems to be situated on or in, or at a vortex where dimensions intersect." I don't know exactly what this means; who does?

A definition of a Vortex (Webster dictionary) is a whirling mass forming a vacuum at its center, into which anything caught in the motion is drawn (moving in a vortex) the explanation certainly seems plausible at the least. Picturing in my mind that we are actually sitting on a vortex has helped me in this way, by increasing my own sensitivity to the paranormal phenomena that surrounds the house.

Sitting in an easy chair one night I began to notice a heavy fragrance that seemed to rush by my face. This made me think of the older refined lady, the perfume lady as I call her. The strange smells were becoming stronger and more often now. Each time I not noticed this fragrance the lamp shade would be moving. I felt with certainty that somehow I would be learning a lot from the other side and with great ambition. This discovery was such an amazing part of my life now.

In the coming weeks I called Beverly on the phone and we had some marvelous talks. She began to teach me about so many things, things I had never heard of. Vortexes, spirit guides, and my spiritual teachers, who she says, "Are sort of assigned to us while we are on earth and in other dimensions."

A Dictionary definition of a dimension is; planes, spheres, plateaus, an example; the fourth dimension is time and space.

But most of all she encouraged me to read, read, read! How grateful I am to her. I have never met anyone even remotely like her. She is in this world but not of this world and on a very high plane and is a very humble person asking for nothing and I know her to be one of my teachers here and always ready to assist me.

After I had a chance to absorb some of this information I called David our son, with news of the visit by Beverly and Chris and the information they had shared. When I told him about how Beverly sensed that she had known him in another lifetime he became very excited and couldn't wait to meet both Beverly and Chris. Since he was not able to come home to meet them right away he decided to call her. Their meeting by phone was a turning point for him, as her visit to my house had been for me.

He was stunned by everything she had related to him. Specifically about some of the experiences he had on his last vacation and generally about himself and his life. I later discovered that Beverly does not divulge information about anyone or to anyone without first obtaining permission from her own guide or guides. The right to privacy is one of her highest directives or priorities. Since that telephone call, Beverly and David have grown increasingly bonded.

Contentment and a sense of peacefulness were increasingly becoming a part of my life even though I now sensed a greater degree of activity in the house. Perhaps the spirits were happy that I, that we all, had more awareness of them. Perhaps one of the reasons for my increased restfulness has directly to do with my decreased interest in material things. We all to be sure tend to worry about whether there will be enough money in our lives and whether or not, we are getting our fair share of respect, love, admiration, etc. But I was caught up in a new world and completely fascinated!

Through the paranormal events in our house I have been introduced to a different perspective, the big picture as I like to put it. Through which our intentions and behavior are of primary importance. Perhaps this thing called life is really very much our school, I call it Earth school. In which we are suppose to figure out just what our purpose is and then attempt to go about fulfilling that purpose. If what I think is the case, turns out to in fact be the case, when we leave this Earth School we will merely be at recess. That is to say, death may not mean graduation from earthly life at all; rather, it may well only be a brief hiatus. With the close of which we will hear the bell sounding those of us back to class. That is what my spirits have taught me or at least inclined me to think. That's why I feel such affection for them and am so grateful for them. I found I soon disliked calling the spirits by the ghost name any longer they were much more than that!

I talked again to Beverly and asked her hundreds of questions. I became more and more convinced that freedom from the past, freedom from the future, freedom from everything that keeps us from living an authentic and core of compassion, is what life is all about. She kept talking to me about how much we as human beings whether we realize it or not are all connected. That connection for me is derived from the increasing sense of compassion, of oneness. I feel this with all living things both dead and alive! It's very comforting to think that we go on and on, being driven by some benevolent force that is both immanent and transcendent. It means there will always be a tomorrow, a bright tomorrow, and that translates into hope and joy for me.

My husband and I had been in bed for a short while one evening not long after he had finished remodeling the kitchen. All of a sudden we both heard approximately fifteen loud hammer banging sounds waking us up! The hammering noises radiated throughout the house from the area of our new kitchen. I began to laugh because I sensed right away that it must have been Joseph giving us a taste of our own medicine, when we were trying to rest! I was finding out that several of our spirit friends's had a great sense of humor and I appreciated it!

For many people the noise would certainly have terrified them in the middle of the night or anytime. That is why I can stress now that the noises are to gain ones attention, it wasn't to harm us.

During that same period I happened to be painting a ceiling when a wonderful idea came to me: why not use our video camera and tape recorder to record kind of any paranormal activity? I went to the store and bought half dozen blank tapes for the video camera and the tape player. I began to walk around the house stopping to record with the tape player first. I was the only one home when I recorded so I knew I would not pick up regular house noises. I was dumbfounded when I played the tapes back. At first I only heard strange things. I could hear people moving about the house! Then heard a drawer open and close. I could hear a screen door opening and closing, we don't have a screen door. There were metal buckets clanking and I could hear a discussion between two adults and a child, Katie no doubt. The voices were muffled so I could not tell what they clearly were saying. The more I went over the tape it appeared to me the tape had recorded *both* dimensions at once! It WAS both theirs and ours, it was all very odd to say the least. The camera would record the sounds of our time and space, but overlapped into events of their time and space. It was very odd indeed and fascinating!

I decided one day to record by our bedroom in the hall which certainly seems to be the heart of the house. I shut the door to the other rooms nearby and turned on the recorder to ask the room a few questions. I paused after each question to allow any spirit who may be there a time to answer. After all, I don't know how much of their energy it takes to make an audible sound. I did not hear any response while I was taping, but when I played the tape back I was shocked! My voice was not my voice! Rather it was a man's voice very low and slow, as if the tape was dragging at the wrong speed. I decided to re-tape just to make sure I wasn't experiencing a mechanical failure. Then I decided to record again only further into the hallway where the burning odor would be from time to time and began.

As soon as the tape was rolling I asked for a sign, "Will I ever see one of you?" With the last word of that sentence out of my mouth the bedroom door in front of me began to move back and forth, increasing in speed until it was vibrating so fast it was nearly a blur and making quite a noise! I turned up the volume setting on the tape player hoping to record the noise. It continued until I worked up the courage to put my hand firmly on the door and stop it! Needless to say I assumed I received an answer to my question. Perhaps, it was one of the spirit men making the door move; perhaps it was something else all I can say with certainty is that the door began vibrating at a terrific speed on its own! When playing the tape again my voice was still that of a deep man!

Incidentally, I have discovered that there may be a good reason why we periodically smell something burning in the hallway just outside our master bedroom upstairs with a reasoning of why Katie seems to occupy that portion of the house more than any other.

The first time I detected smoke it was in the middle of the night. I bolted out of bed thinking the house was on fire! I have since discovered there use to be a chimney running up from an old parlor fireplace right where the upstairs hallway is now. We believe that Katie, whose gravestone I have found in the area dating her death on December 21, 1867 had much to do with this. She may of been have been laid-out at her funeral near the old fireplace downstairs in our house. Katie did live here at that time and I have seen the family name on our deed.

When my son and were led by Katie we found her gravestone it merely reads Katie, she appears to be buried near her family members. When we stood there beside Katie' grave I suddenly felt drawn that we should take a picture as I stood beside her stone. When I had the film developed I was surprised to see a wide stream of bright, gold light coming from the sky across my body to the ground! I could only hold the tears back and say "thank you Katie." So now, I knew for sure that the smell of smoke in our house was one of Katie's ways of saying "I'm here!" She identifies herself in this way.

Having experienced my first encounter on tape I couldn't help but remember what Beverly had said, "that the spirits could move back and forth freely between our space-time and theirs." I feel so fortunate that from every indication all these spirits are about love. I cannot speak with any experience whatever about any other kind. Perhaps a review of all my spiritual friends would be in order, and in addition I will introduce some I have not yet mentioned.

THE SLAVE: Who appears as an older man with graying hair and an average build or perhaps smaller. I get the feeling that he is still hurting from the hardships he had to endure during his earthly life. He apparently left the kitchen area one night and passed through our bedroom, paying no attention to us. He was in solid form heading towards the staircase that leads back downstairs as he walked past our bed. I felt he was just going through his regular route doing whatever he did in life here. He paid no attention to us at all.

THE LUMBERJACK: Is very tall and with a very large build. He sports a moustache, beard and wears a plaid shirt. I remember when we began to notice his very large footprints in the carpets around the house. We measured them and to our astonishment his foot is fifteen inches long, and seven inches wide! I have several pictures that I have taken of his footprints in the carpet. We still joke about not wanting to ever make him angry!

QUEENIE: Who is proud, stately, and slim. We think she was the overseer of the house, and I guess still is! She loves where she is, and as Beverly told me, "no one has the right to force anyone to do anything." So she stays where she wants to be, not bothering anyone.

FOLDING LADY: This spirit loves to fold and pleat articles of all kinds, towels, washcloths, bedspreads, doilies, and so forth. She may have been a maid. She seems to watch over little Katie with tender care. She shows much evidence of her hand-work in our home.

KATIE JANE: A beautiful child, small boned with curly light brown hair who usually wears a large grin on her chubby face. She is still five years old to her and enjoys wearing a white dress and hair ribbons. Katie appears to be a very happy and radiant being and she loves where she is.

THE LIBRARY TABLE SCHOOLTEACHER: She comes and goes a lot. I know her name is Nicky. She likes to check on her table. She obviously loved her table very much and must have graded a great number of tests and essays, and written many letters there. We think her husband worked for the railroad, was jealous and carried a gun. Nicky is quite young, has blond hair, is very pretty, and was a schoolteacher. Beverly has picked up all of this information and the word divorce three times when she has felt into this spirit. Perhaps she divorced her husband or perhaps he killed her before she got the chance since she did die so young.

GARAGE MAN: Loves to watch the progress Leon is making on rehabilitating the house. My husband has several times misplaced a board he was cutting, only to look above him and see it perched up high across a tree limb some five feet above his head!

Also, the lights in the garage often turn on and off by themselves and the door is found closed when it was left open, and vise-versa. One day I had just finished sweeping the garage floor clean only to turn around to find paint sticks on the floor. They had not been there a moment before --- spelling out the word 'Hi!" And when we return at night sometimes before we drive in the lights are turned on for us in both the garage and the house, welcoming us back home. I always try to remember to say,"'thank you." This gentle man obviously loves his little pranks and wants to be helpful. At Christmas time the inside and outside Christmas lights are on including the window candles when we return home! The spirits must also love this time of the year.

Another phenomenon I have encountered in my house is a series of colored balls of lights. The first time I began to see them I was in the kitchen with Leon. They floated out of the wall and moved towards me and seemed to dissolve into me. I was so excited that I exclaimed to

Leon, "Can you see them, Can you see them?" He looked at me saying, "What?" At this point I began to realize that I could see many things that perhaps were not visible to everyone. Leon had the look of "oh no, what does she see now?" I was later told this sort of vision is called *"second sight"* and that it allows one to see into other dimensions. I was excited needless to say!

Perhaps I was raising my vibration level or however one refers to spiritual growth. Also around this time I began to catch glimpses of one of the spirit ladies in her long dresses going into another room. She seemed to be accompanied by little orbs of pink and green lights and I would see sparkles of lights in blues, gold, white, and orchid. I was completely fascinated to say the least. I told Leon I could just hear the doctor asking, "Now how long have you been seeing these things?"

I would at times be in the kitchen and the refrigerator door would be open when I turned around! The egg tray would be balanced precariously off the refrigerator shelf where it had been previously been tucked in neatly. Items began to get moved about more and more, and transported upstairs sometimes. One day while I was vacuuming I came across a big lump under the rug precisely where we walk most of the time. I bent down and pulled up the throw rug to find my new sewing scissors! Every day now was amazing to me...

Only Leon and I were living in the house by this time, and I am very particular about keeping things in their place. For instance, if I had the thought I wanted to read before I went to bed a few times I found my reading glasses already placed by my bedside! Since the light is not good in the bedroom I don't usually read very often there. It was a treat to find the glasses brought to me by one of our spirit friends. There also came a day while I was dusting and noticed that a large oriental figurine was missing from the mantle and to this day it has not shown up. I usually have items returned to me, I will look up one day and there the item will be. Various items seem to come and go… I look at it as only being borrowed for whatever reason. There were times my son found mine in his home!

Another example was my son's silver antique sugar bowl. It had been in the front parlor for months while we were redoing our kitchen. Moving things back into the room I was excited putting the finishing touches on the arrangement of furniture. Looking over the kitchen area I was wondering what I could set on the old wooden oak table that we use for breakfast. Then I thought of David' beautiful antique sugar bowl! I went to get it in the parlor only to find that the collection of spoons that fit around it was missing! I KNEW they had been there! I was puzzled, but thought perhaps I imagined it and David had somehow stored the spoons with him for some reason. I stepped back into the kitchen with an armload of items. Two minutes later I returned to get the sugar bowl and there were ALL of the spoons! All eleven of them tucked neatly in their places around the sugar bowl! I remember being so excited and whirling around shouting, "Oh, I can't believe it!" I was so excited that I felt a little faint. I marveled at how our friendly spirits could always seem to read my thoughts. I was alone in the house that day and had not verbalized any of my plans for putting the finishes touches on the kitchen. Our spirits seem to be helping me in their way.

It was at that time that I became absolutely convinced that though the spirits in the house were sometimes fond of playing practical jokes, they were basically even fonder of being helpful. I felt a closer kinship to them and my heart sent out love to all of them. All the objects moving and falling, the voices, the sounds and marks of footprints, all were designed to get our attention. To sort of say, "We're here, and we are your friends." I felt a lot of joy due to all these encounters --- so much to learn about! Yes, I only had good feelings about this house, not in spite of the strangeness but because of it.

I do remember back to one day before the kitchen area was completed when the slave was still upset with all the commotion. I had bought a small, beautiful antique table for our house and had temporarily placed it very near the door leading to the kitchen. I wanted to decide exactly where I wanted to place it. We came home a few evenings later to find one leg of the table broken off and the table lying on its side on the floor! I could have cried. I had placed several fragile glass items on the table which were all intact. They were sitting perfectly upright on the floor beside the table, as if they were placed there by hand! Subsequently to that time I placed another table in that spot near the kitchen and it too was suddenly found to have a broken leg! For whatever reason someone does not like anything in that spot or because the spirits move about with such great *speed* they can unknowingly move things without intent. I believe the latter idea of the movement knowing they do not harm or break items with intent. The speed of energy is with a great force.

My table story above brings to mind the day we purchased new faucet handles for the kitchen sink. They were packed in a box wrapped with tissue paper around them. I was in the next room when all of a sudden I heard paper rattling. I went to see what it was in the kitchen and the sound stopped abruptly! I returned to my chore at hand and soon I heard the sound again. The third time I knew without a doubt it had be the paper in the faucet box. I slowly sneaked up close to the box as it rustled again, just in time to see paper moving! When I asked Beverly what had happened she said, "The one garage man here was only curious by trying to look into the box. He was curious since he was not familiar with modern plumbing fixtures." This made perfect sense! My world had really changed and I loved my school lessons.

I encountered more and more phenomena and I became more and more comfortable with it. I began to make connections. I began to associate the tape recorder I made of the sounds in the house to where in the house there seemed to be the most activity. I remembered the first time my voice on the tape sounded like that of a deep throated man. I decided the location where I had recorded on that day might be the lumberjacks' favorite place in the house, in the west bedroom. I was figuring things out to the best I could. In the kitchen I had again recorded the sound of the metal buckets clanging together, doors opening and closing, water being poured out of pails, drawers opening, footsteps on wooden floors, we do not have wooden floors in the house.

Recorded also was "whispering" noises, the sound of paper being rustled and moved about, and as if a heavy piece of furniture was being pulled across the floor! My husband and I began to accept the idea that the spirits here were probably going about their everyday tasks as they had done in their normal lives. I couldn't help but notice that Leon was getting more unsettled and edgy, even though he knew they are of a positive nature. Things didn't affect me the same way; I felt strongly there would be a big reason why all of this was happening. I of course can't say exactly what they were and are doing.

With what I have had explained from my dear friend Beverly I feel comfortable with the notion that the spirits are just doing their usual tasks. At night when I leave the recorder on things can get extremely noisy in the kitchen, after all they do not have time as we do on the other side in their dimension. Ordinary noise is generally quieter at night and thus I think the spirits just seem noisier at night. One noise in particular did give us a panic, it sounded as though something very heavy was being dragged across a wooden floor, like a heavy trunk being moved from upstairs, and at times we heard a sniff or sigh!

One day I was busy in the kitchen when I felt someone near me, whirling around I saw the utility doors open! I sensed the folding lady so I took a picture of her and the doors moving. You can see the shoot off in the picture of what I call her "arm" opening the doors in this picture. She has led many lives…It's never a dull moment and wonderful to have so much evidence of life after life!

I would try not to laugh when Leon began experiencing an increasingly number of things for himself. One evening we were going out for awhile. He turned off the lamp before we left. He walked a few steps away toward the front door and all of a sudden it popped back on! He turned it off a second and third time and the same thing happened! Apparently someone wanted to get his attention! He just looked very strange --- he can shake his head with the best of them without moving a muscle.

Most nights when the noises from the street and the neighborhood get quiet I notice the commotion starts, dishes and glassware in the kitchen are rattling and clinking. Respectively as if they are preparing a meal of their own! When our son David visits, the next morning he sometimes laughs and says, "Boy, were they all noisy last night! I couldn't get a wink of sleep with them clanking around the kitchen all night." We would laugh so much about our experiences. It certainly seems there is no concept of time or at least a different concept of time --- in dimensions' of the spirits. I suppose that is one thing certain the spirits never need to be concerned with. They are living in their dimension.

One evening Leon went into the kitchen from the garage. I followed him a minute or two later after I had finished doing a chore. When I entered the kitchen and saw him standing there I stopped short: He looked as white as a sheet standing completely still as though he had entered the Twilight Zone or something. I asked him "what was wrong" and he said, "You won't believe this but when I came in the kitchen two men were talking right here by the counter! I couldn't see anyone and though the voices were loud they were muffled to so I couldn't tell what was being said."

What is strange about this happening to him is that he has a hearing loss from his work. But in our home he was able to see and hear the spirits here.

While in the kitchen I heard the laundry doors opening (at right) I turned in time to see this spirit opening a door. I quickly used my camera to capture this photo. See the darker offshoot which is the spirit (arm) opening the door.

This was the first time he had actually heard voices since the time he had actually heard the two female spirits he hoped was my daughter and me coming home one day. I would understate things when I say that it certainly left a lasting impression on him.

One day after this I was sitting outside on the porch enjoying the sunshine and thinking of how our lives had changed. The neighbor man walked over to talk with Leon. They were standing not far away from the porch. We had a large ladder up against a tree that went to the roof of the porch. I began to hear a thump, then repeated thumping. Looking to my left side I was shocked at where the noise was coming from. The heavy ladder was beating the tree back and forth! I felt sure Leon and the man would be shocked as well but they seemed to not hear the noise. All I supposed was I was to notice this event for some reason. I felt the garage/handy man spirit was getting my attention. This was a heavy long ladder! As suddenly as it started it stopped! I realized then I could see and hear very well now in their other world and perhaps this was another of my lessons to prepare me more.

On another day later on I found the newspaper in the house beside Leon's chair! Wow, now the paper has been brought in for him! It never happened again but it did on that one day. I know the children must of been wondering what was next. I thought how sweet, how caring, I could not believe it, but it happened and was happening! I felt guilty our spirits were still with us but they did with their free will.

The month of May came and around Memorial Day our son came home and was finally going to meet Beverly for himself. We all decided to meet halfway in a store that was owned by a friend of Beverly's. On the way David said, "I will know her when I see her; we will know each other so don't tell me what she looks like." We arrived first and I went to another part of the store so he would not be distracted. Beverly arrived, came in, looked- over at him and David at her. They went into each other's arms and hugged in greeting. Old souls together again, I thought, it was just as they both said it would be.

We went to a restaurant to have lunch and were joined by another friend of Beverly's. Upon meeting this person I was overjoyed to see my first aura, which is the energy field that surrounds all things. We happened at the time to be talking about auras and Beverly asked me "what color my son's was?" I told her "I didn't physically see his aura." "But you know what color it is, don't you?" "Gold" I answered. Somehow I just knew. She smiled and said "yes." Then she asked me to tell her what color her friends' aura was. I looked at her friend and for some reason I could see a beautiful pale blue light glowing about her. I was so happy: I could see her aura! From that time on I have regularly perceived particular shades of light surrounding people. I had no idea I was using one of my given gifts.

I once again was so grateful to have met Beverly. I wish that I had met her a long time ago so I could have been set upon this path earlier in my life. I mentioned this to her once and she replied, "No, please don't feel that way because the time is only right for you now in your life." After that comment I remembered earlier on when the angel said, "When the pupil is ready the teacher will come." Again, everything evolves the way it should. All of us move through our trials and errors, all kinds of things really while we are here. That is why I am working on letting go of the worries, the fears, and the guilt, as best I can. In its place is more love, compassion, and forgiveness. So my own personal experiencing of auras began that day, and later I would come to understand much more on how aura's are derived from the way we happen to be made. They are reflected in the colors we choose to wear and things we buy, and they are always present in our health and illness. The aura tells what we are in personality and our feelings. The aura is a magnificent tool of what one is of that we each have. I would come to see auras more and use this information in my healing work in the near future. Things like this had never entered my mind, but I was finding out that everything is connected in many intricate and intimate ways.

CHAPTER TWO
Major Experiences and Hidden Lives

Katie Jane continues to be present most of the time. On many nights she is present on our bed in the wee hours. I did not tell Leon about her nightly proximity. She stayed on my side of the bed anyway. One night however, he turned in before I did (a rare occurrence) and when I finally came to bed he sat up and said, "I hope it's finally you this time!" I knew right then he had met Katie and I couldn't keep from laughing. I told him how I had spared him from her nightly visits until she saw fit to introduce herself to him. I just figured that because of her tragic death at the hands of her father she might wish to take her time getting to know Leon.

She must have taken a liking to him fairly quickly because not long after that when I was away from the house; Leon was working upstairs and heard female voices. They seemed to be mostly laughing and giggling. He thought I had returned to the house with our youngest daughter and he hoped (with all his heart!) that he was right! As he crept down the stairs to locate and hopefully identify the voices the house was still empty! I told him upon my return that Katie was probably with one of the other female spirits who watches over her and not to worry. Leon looked as if to say, "not to worry!" He explained that to be awakened out of a nice sleep with something moving about his feet was a concern to him! And in order to get his rest was another issue. Now with the strange voices that he could hear was another matter for him. He had no control any of this either I knew he was thinking what will we do? I was becoming more concerned about Leon I was fine with things but he certainly wasn't and I suppose most people would feel as he did.

I soon discovered that one of our spirits does not like air-conditioning or maybe it was the speed with which they traveled. It was beginning to create a problem around our window unit on most nights after we turned on our unit. We would hear a loud crash followed by what sounded like heavy objects falling down the stairs! We kept two heavy objects on top of the unit to keep the curtains away from the flow of air. The items in question, upon our investigation of the noise, would invariably be off the unit and on the stairs, or all the way into the front parlor below.

This movement of the objects went on all summer long that year and occurred sometimes when the unit was off! I have wondered if the movement of the objects is always purposeful, or whether, because the spirits seem to be constituted more by energy matter? Perhaps, if at times the movement of the spirits automatically sucks matter along with them. It is much like a racecar driver who follows closely behind their competitors taking advantage of the vacuum created by the car in front of them. Whatever the case may be Beverly says, "our house is certainly a vortex."

This is how the dictionary describes it, "a route without time, a swirling mass forming a vacuum at its center into which anything caught in the motion is drawn, or is aligned with, or situated upon a vortex." And, the center is defiantly in our master bedroom, bathroom and hall upstairs.

A vortex can bring many things in and out of that area. That could be the reason for so much activity in our house. David has said, "He senses the most activity there, and perhaps this area of the house is in fact a portal, a threshold, through which the spirits pass back and forth from their dimension and ours." In any event, Beverly has said, "that this is the most active house she has ever encountered but it is good and from high planes."

The other side had to do something to open me up to gain my attention, so I could begin to learn about my life's work. Finding out I was not only here to be a mother and give my children an upbringing but I have a lot more to do. For all of this I am humbly grateful.

I began to discover much more about myself as I became more familiar with the paranormal activity in our house. I seem for instance, to find myself talking an increasing amount to the recently departed I have known in this life and others. Sometimes in our conversations I would be saying, "You've been dead a year now" to a spirit. And then continue to address topics or people with which the deceased and I were familiar. Often upon checking the calendar I found that I had struck these conversations on the exact anniversary of their death. One friend of mine for example, had died very young at the age of 39. I remember when she came to visit me and began telling me of the spiritual work she was busy doing on the other side. She looked wonderful, younger than she did at the time of her death, as the spiritual presence of a deceased individual nearly always appears to me. I take this to convey to me that they are healthy and happy, no worries or fears. They can come as they wish and at whatever age they wish to appear.

How wonderful that I am learning from all of this and getting a look into the other side as well. Such encounters have evolved into experiencing something related, namely the experiencing of some of my own past-lives. A past-life is also something I am being taught about, something I had not really thought about before.

The dictionary definition of a past-life is, lives lived previously; this has been proven under hypnosis, previous past life experiences. This is also a good place to explain Spirit. A spirit is indestructible life, meaning that the essence of the individual never dies. We never die our souls go on eternally. It is life after life. I know what I am relating to you the reader, may sound like nonsense.

But though I cannot be certain exactly what I am experiencing and writing about here, I nevertheless am certain that it is not nonsense. Everything has meaning; all is interconnected I had never heard of most of these things --- vortexes, dimensions, and self movement of objects, past lives, and so forth. But here I was living them more and more all the time.

Continuing with regard to past lives I have been shown my son and me in Egypt and the experience was particularly strong. I was a male warrior of some kind in line behind other warriors waiting to do something when my turn came. As I moved forward I began to see what I was supposed to do: we carried scimitars and in front of us was a small temple. There in front of it were Buddhist monks sitting on the ground. The warrior in front of me in the line was preparing to do his duty, when it was his turn he went running with a bloodcurdling scream to the closest monk. The Monk sat with head bowed, meditating or praying, and the Warrior with a wide swing of his sword cut off the monks' head! I was horrified; I would never take a life! I planned to sneak away during all the outbursts of cries. When I began to try slipping away from my duty however, two other warriors quickly discovered me! In punishment for my cowardice or treason they held me against a tree and beheaded me! I felt the sword coming and I felt, well my quick immediate passing. I only knew that I did the right thing! I had no regrets...

Experiencing past lives in this way is not like dreaming, though you may accuse yourself of dreaming if you like. There is a vast difference between dreaming and past-life experiences. The latter is much more lucid, three-dimensional and interactive. You are there much more than when you are merely dreaming. I was to be shown many other life times and all of these lessons would become clear to me later on.

I have always had a great love for the film Gone with the Wind, especially for the characters Rhett and Scarlett. During a time of quiet meditation, of relaxation call it what you like, I entered this movie in which I have had a great if unexplained fondness. All of a sudden I was in a lovely gown, dancing on the ballroom floor. Dancing has played a big part in my current life. I have danced on stage professionally for many different occasions, competition during my early years. I even called my mom and dad Rhett and Scarlett, if just to myself. They looked like their doubles, two of them would be cornered on vacation with people thinking the two of them were Vivian Lee and Clark Gable. My mother being so petite with her black curly hair was a double look alike for the movie star Scarlett and dad looked like a double for Rhett with his black hair, same build and dimples.

As I was concentrating on past lives one evening I had a vision where suddenly I saw my parents in an old picture. There they were so in love with each other. My dad was staring adoringly into mother's eyes. I have never encountered this photograph but have no doubt that it existed at one time. I also believe this was a double message, in this way they were showing me of their great love for each other still.

In another vision I saw my parents during what must have been the era of the Civil War. I thought long and hard on these things and perhaps the past life experiences are being facilitated by someone on the other side and our loved ones. I knew I was ready to experience such things or it wouldn't be happening to me.

I believe many of us become guardians, spiritual guides, teachers, and companions, though I don't have a clue why we become one or the other for now. Although I am sure we choose this with our free will. Perhaps, a human being who dies after a lingering illness or disability may enjoy a period of rest before their work begins.

Again, who knows but this is the direction I have been set in by the beings of light, and the angels. In any event as a spirit once told me, "We all have various jobs to do over here; we don't just sit around! That would be a dreadful waste wouldn't it?" So this is what I believe that we go on helping others and choosing what we want to do. To be able to help others is a great and wonderful thing on this side or the other.

I have experienced spirits telling me of how some of them work with children who are crossing over and others who help with our pet's crossing over. I was getting confirmations that our pets were sent here as precious gifts' to comfort and love us with all their hearts, and are loving companions to us. They are sent as a great gift to us in our lives to also help us, we must respect them and give them the best we can. I have always believed that pets' have a special purpose and they do have a soul! This information came from the other side.

We have a little angel companion who stays close to my son. She is the most loving, faithful companion ever and always beside him all through his illness. I will tell you how I met this very special little angel early on.

I happily greeted David when he came home for a visit and the first thing he said was, "Mom, I know you don't have pets in the house but I have something to show you. It's just for the week-end and if you don't want me to do this I know something else I can do." With that he pulled the zipper down a few inches on his winter jacket and out popped the sweetest, tiny face I have have ever seen, a little miniature Yorkie dog with long blond hair! As I looked into those big brown eyes I felt as if I was looking into my old dogs eyes I had when I was growing up as a child. I felt a big connection and I fell in love with this little angel that David had brought home. There would be many times that she would prove herself as to her earthly mission here. Not that little Shorty had to prove anything all she needed was us to love her and that was an instant emotion the moment anyone saw her. I would later come to understand why Shorty was so tied to David and all of us I adored her!

That brings to mind of how many people don't believe animals have a soul. I certainly don't try to change one's view on these things but in my case the other side and Christ like Beings has let me know they do. Without a doubt this is what I believe with all my being. I would never doubt the information and goodness that is related to me from the other side. I have no idea about animals other than dogs, cats, and horses, because that is all I have been taught about so far and have seen in visions. But I don't think a line was drawn on what or who was created.

Speaking of souls, Beverly told me that when she worked in hospitals as a nurse and was attending the bedside of dying patients the room often would be filled with spiritual beings waiting to help that person cross over. After Beverly told me this, I too, at a later date would be aware of such divine assistance when someone is close to death. The aura around the person would begin to break-up and start to leave their life form up through the crown. This meant the loved one was close to joining those waiting for him or her. I am always awed by the emotions I sense at such moments.

As I said in the Introduction, the underlying purpose I have in writing this book does not have to do merely with the occurrences and episodes herein described. Rather, my purpose concerns the Big Picture, which is all about love and compassion. I have been taught it is the journey we take that is the most important, not the end. If the loving spirits in my house had not awakened me I would possibly still be in the throes of anxiety, worry, and fear of being a human being. I suppose it is possible to be made more anxious, worried, and afraid by such paranormal encounters, but such has not been my experience. I have learned to understand that fear is something that we create ourselves. It is certainly natural to be afraid of what one cannot see, but know is there anyway. It is at least just as natural to not be afraid and to use the situation as a springboard toward learning about the Big Picture. This has to do with love and compassion and nothing else.

I have learned not to be afraid in my own home, even if I feel what I consider to be a negative energy attempting to put its roots down here. At those times I tell the energy and myself that I am the owner of this house, that it is my place of residence, and that it is not permitted to stay! Only positive energies are welcome in my home. If you let something scare you to death, it just may even if it is alive but invisible

--- feed off your fears and thereby grow. Don't let it! You are the one in control so stand your ground.

I feel somewhat validated in this conclusion because of a telephone conversation I had last summer with a couple that are famous for exorcising houses of negative energy. The wife told me after studying our house for a day or two (with the aid of photographs I had sent her) that all was positive and good in my home. There was nothing negative here. She said, "They would like to come and study this house since it was so different than others they had encountered, which were so contaminated with negativity and fear. Ours was good and positive.

This famous couple is highly respected in the field of paranormal encounters and I hope to have them stay with us for a few days in the future. They were a second confirmation on the house being very positive and good. The thing with sitting located on a vortex means too, that many things could pass in and out. Sometimes a negative energy could enter as well as the positive. Keeping in mind of how to handle this is the key. I know the spirits that are here in this house would certainly not want any negative energy here. Who knows why some spirits are positive in nature and others are negative? I believe however that intentionally is central, and that it carries-over upon death into the other side. But I also believe that such post-mortem energy must be invited into your life, whether consciously or unconsciously. Inviting the negative seems to me too often to be the way of cults, of devil-worship, and perhaps Ouija Boards. I feel that energy whether positive or negative, tends to linger on this plane even after death.

If a negative person had occupied a house for example, I'm sure many of you would upon entering that house feel very uncomfortable. I think it's easier to perceive negative energy after one has practiced being positive, at least this has been the case for me. The negative energies seem to feed from the positive ones if the positive ones let them, so I tend to either steer clear of persons who are oriented toward the negative or else not allow their negativity to embrace me, if I cannot steer clear of them. Why not expect the best --- the most positive --- in any and every situation? Some of us are raised it seems to look for the worst, to expect to fail, and to in fact be afraid. Why not release oneself from all that and just be positive, freed, from any mundane notion of failure and think of success. Why not take each moment as it comes, living to the fullest with as much good will as we can muster?

Yes I know, such a break from conditioned ways of thinking and feeling and doing is not easy --- believe me, I've been there. It is however, altogether possible. Believe me on this score as well, we all don't deserve suffering it is just a natural part of life. What we do deserve is the best, the most compassionate, the most positive outlook, an outlook that has been freed from fear! We all have a choice because Christ gives us all free will. Although suffering and fear can and do overlap, they don't always. Being positive means to not identify yourself with your sufferings as though you are being punished; rather, when you let go of the fear and guilt suffering becomes profound, even transcendent, an experience that gives way to the transcendence of meaninglessness. Everything is connected and everything has meaning. And above all, there is nothing --- nothing to be afraid of in the big picture.

I believe that we have all been allowed a certain amount of time each time around on this earth. I also believe that we all have selected our parents, our earthly contexts, in which to learn additional things. When we have learned these lessons and filled our life's mission, it's time to leave. Death is not something to mourn as though a separation has occurred. In a real sense, there is no such thing as separation. It is we who have invented this illusion, which is derived from things like ignorance and fear. It is generated from a mind clouded by negativity, by a reluctance to in fact release negativity. Everything is addictive, not incidentally, even the negativity of fear, anxiety, guilt, and shame. It may not seem easy to release such emotions, but we can do it and I believe we have a cheering section on the other side that has actually been assigned to assisting us in doing precisely this task.

Whenever I encounter a particularly rough period or situation, I ask my spiritual teachers and guides to help. One technique I use to relax into such prayer or meditation is counting backwards slowly, visualizing each number or object along the way. I then imagine a spiral going upwards, raising through the ceiling, and the roof until I am in the middle of the universe. I calm my mind, let go of everything, and wait for any words of assistance to come and/or any pictures I may see in my mind's eye. The trick is to get quiet, use your imagination in whatever way you are drawn, and go into yourself. It took me some time to be able to shut down my mind, but I just kept trying to clear it. It takes some time to achieve meditation but the results are wonderful.

Such prayer or meditation is very powerful because it has released the illusions of separation that we have created on this earthly plane. In seeking assistance, you connect yourself. You reintegrate yourself. You experience what really is, namely, a radical interrelatedness of everything and everyone.

Prayer is that powerful: It goes straight to the universe to our higher self, to our Universal Father, Christ. Prayer when identified as such is total goodness in all dimensions and honors all. I have concluded that the soul, the spirit of the personality if you will, can travel faster than thought or so at least it seems. Everything is easier, painless, and timeless on the other side: no greed, no jealously, no illness.

To be sure, I also believe that we are allowed to review our life on earth to assess our contributions and our weaknesses. Perhaps this may be what hell is all about and being allowed to connect back with our physical existence even when we have become detached from it. I believe the earthly plane is the school, and death marks the beginning of recess, at which time and in which place, we begin to heal from the time of entrenchment on earth. While I, in no fashion wish to be interpreted as supplying answers to questions that are for all intents and purposes impenetrable for us, at least during earthly life. Perhaps all the vast puzzles of life, babies dying, genetic diseases, natural catastrophes that kill hundreds, suicides, and so forth, have to do with the lessons that we learn, or do not learn, or have already learned in a past life while here on earth. And most astounding of all, perhaps such sorrows of life actually do involve, in some fashion defies logic, the free will of those concerned.

Perhaps we choose to enter this life again with a disease, or destined to die young or be involved in a natural disaster or to direct us onto a path of despair. We, choose perhaps such hardships of life from the distance and perspective of the other side. In order to meet out good results in the form of lessons or experiences needed. And for that matter, perhaps we sometimes choose to stick around after death, in the form of a spiritual presence that haunts a particular location. Maybe at times we need to be ghosts in order to take care of some unfinished business that otherwise would go attended. Who can say for sure, but because of the spirits I have been set on a course to think on such things. I ponder the Big Picture and as a result the worries of the mundane world hold much less fascination for me with regard to the unlimited free will that I believe we all have.

I would like to tell you a true story about a dear friend of my Aunt who lived in the southwest part of the United States. The story begins when my Aunt Louise moved into a new apartment. As she was carrying a box into her apartment she was greeted by a nice middle-aged man welcoming her to the neighborhood. Even though Aunt Louise is deaf, she can read lips. She at first noticed something different about him, and as time went on she began to recognize something that can only be described as familiar about him. Her feeling seemed odd since they had never met before. As time passed their friendship grew and then a dating relationship began. In the process of their courtship, Mike the gentleman, started to reveal some very interesting things to her about him.

He only told her a little at a time so she would not be startled or frightened away. He told her how he had been here on earth many times, and that they had been together before in previous lifetimes. He had recognized her immediately when he saw her move in, and that his awareness of their relationships in previous lives had been the reason for his friendly greeting. He said, "He was a teacher both on this side and on the other and that at times they would be together when he might be called away suddenly, and for her not to worry about his sudden departure." He explained, "he didn't always know what he was being called to do, and wouldn't know until he arrived at the place he was being drawn to." She took this with an open mind and because she was so drawn to him. She knew his heart was true.

Then one day Mike told Aunt Louise that he was to build a house up in the mountains. Soon he had dug the foundation by hand and hauled in rock in his own truck to pave a road leading to the house. Then he built the house never telling Aunt Louise the reason for his compulsive construction project. Soon to Aunt Louise's horror, he said, "he would be going away, leaving this earth in a short time --- in which, he would be going home as he put it to the other side." One day not long after this discussion he was found dead of a heart attack! I recall Aunt Louise telling me that Mike had told her in confidence he had been here so many times, and hoped this time he could stay and work on the other side. I found this story of Mike confirming my thoughts and lessons about the hereafter. My dear Aunt being an enlightened soul was gracious enough to tell me this beautiful story and I will always thank her for it.

His death was not the only tragedy that Aunt Louise has experienced in her life. As I said, she is almost totally deaf and her first marriage failed when she was middle aged. For a long time she didn't really know what to do with herself but slowly she began to pick up the pieces of her life. She began by developing a special program to help the handi-capped and low-income individuals and families. She reached out, in other words and by doing so reached inside herself. She has no advanced degrees --- only a high school diploma--- but because of her dream to help others, and her persistence, people who were in a position to assist her in implementing them accepted her ideas. She *never* gave up on her plan. In short, she was able to transform her despair into a realized dream; the bad into something very positive not only for herself but also for many others and she helped many people.

And along the way she met Sonny, a wonderful gentleman, and she contemplated entering another bliss filled marriage. Sonny treated her like royalty, and they shared a deep, abiding love for each other. He would take her on trips and encourage her to try new techniques and technologies to increase her ability to hear. Wedding plans were laid, but before the happy event he called us in the heartland and asked, "If we would pick him up at the airport since he had business in the area." We were very eager to see him again and he stayed with us for two days. The last time I saw Sonny was in our car, pulling out of the driveway as Leon drove him back to the airport at the conclusion of his business. I noticed he was all smiles as usual that day, but I saw in him a great tiredness, a great weariness. He was concerned about Aunt Louise and couldn't wait to get back to her, especially since she was feeling rather ill and couldn't make this trip with him. In a very short time we got the sad call from a close friend: Sonny had died suddenly also from a heart attack and my aunt felt alone in the world again. And yet, she continued to put herself to the task of assisting the needy people in her programs. Several years later at her retirement party she was honored by hundreds of people including major CEOs of companies. It was because despite her tragedies --- or perhaps because of them --- she had continued to care about others.

Aunt Louise is thus a great teacher. She recently came to visit us and I for some reason felt comfortable telling her about my experiences. Not surprisingly, she was very receptive to my stories and even met Beverly during her visit. While the four of us (David was here too) were visiting, I kept seeing a male spirit in the room with us but couldn't quite make out his face, even though I had a good idea who he was. I told my aunt that this man was present and that he was smiling all the while we were talking. Beverly had seen him also and told us it was Sonny. He wanted to tell Aunt Mary he would always love her and that he is often near to her, and protecting her. That afternoon I took a photograph of Beverly, Aunt Louise and David. When the picture was developed there appeared right beside Aunt Louise a gold tinted outline of a tall man whom we have no doubt is Sonny! My aunt treasures this photo. I was thrilled that he appeared in the photograph, but I wasn't surprised.

I had seen Sonny in spirit form right after he died, and he spoke to me about several things, then he laughed and let me know he was just fine! The good part now was I could share this with my dear aunt. Sonny loves her so much and they will always be together in some sense, and I get the strong feeling he will be waiting for her on the other side, and he is watching over her now.

Speaking of taking pictures, the results of my own efforts at photography around this time has been nothing short of baffling. Many pictures I take and with different cameras has obvious strange things in them. I have collected hundreds of them. Also, my collection of tapes from my recorder and video camera is equally astounding. Beverly thinks Hollywood would "kill for them" and would be hard pressed to duplicate anything of their sort with the most advanced computer software. These are all very private to me; someday I may do something with them to give the public a look for themselves.

The first time in my home that I was actually allowed to see one of my spiritual teachers SOLID he gave me his name! I was so overwhelmed that words cannot explain my emotions. Apparently, he is the guide who stays with me all or at least most of the time. I will tell more of how he introduced himself to me later on. He is a very wise strong and gentle spiritual being. Another of my guides is an Indian shaman, who is very intense looking and it is he from whom I draw my courage and strength.

I was at my son David's home in Oklahoma and that night upon retiring I fell deeply asleep. I somehow knew I was traveling into a vision. Suddenly, my Indian Shaman was shown to me very clearly. He was on the most beautiful white horse, his long black hair flying in the wind and held a Lance in his one hand. The colors he wore and the feathers in his hair were extremely beautiful. I watched him in my vision ride back and forth on his horse. I was awake seeing this vision, and yet I couldn't believe my eyes! This magnificent spiritual being was so beautiful I couldn't take my eyes off of him! He wanted me to know him, and by the colors he wore so I would remember this, it was important! It was he who warned me to ignore any forces or persons of negativity that would attempt to impede my growth. I knew I was to call upon him when I needed more strength, and he would always be with me. I watched him until I became very tired, and came out of the vision. I had his name now and felt great comfort with his amazing introduction to me! I was so in awe of my new spirit friends from the other side and the way we were working together!

With respect to my unsympathetic friends, one day while looking in the closet an old Bible we had found years ago in the attic fell out onto my foot. It was lying opened to a certain page; I had stumbled across these words: "Cast not your pearls before swine, lest they trample them beneath their feet." While I don't interpret swine in a pejorative fashion, I was comforted by this verse. Which I did take to refer to those in whom I confided, but have not understood my experiences and turned my friendship away.

It was July, 1992 when I read this passage. The very next day when I was attending a psychic fair I met a wonderful reader named John Paxton. As I sat down at his table (he was the only one I was drawn to so I knew he was the right one) he began by writing a message onto a piece of paper. As I began to read this message John had written down it said, "Cast not your pearls before swine, lest they trample them beneath their feet. Do not give messages to people who are not ready to hear them. It is hard to become separated from old ways and negative friends, but it is for your growth as well as theirs. This does not stop the flow of love, for it always remains strong in your heart." John signed the message: from your Shaman! Then he said, "you know who your Shaman is, don't you? You receive your strength from this loved one and he is a guide to you." I was quite shocked to say the least since I had not said a word yet to him about anything! I immediately thought back to the night my Shaman introduced himself to me in the vision giving me basically the same message!

John went on to tell me several exact occurrences that were going on in my life. He used correct names and places as I sat there not saying anything, and quite in awe of this man. I left by thanking him when he finished his reading for me with the intention to come back the next time he returned. It never happened, because sometime later I sadly learned John had crossed over. Shortly after, he appeared to me in my home in a solid form to give me more messages for some others and myself.

T o explain his visit one night I awoke late at night to see John standing at the top of the stairs in my room and he began speaking to me again and this was one of the messages I cherish most: "Your strength is mighty, straight as the arrow. As you begin your special journey make your mark upon the quest." At that time I had no idea I had been drawn to John by a past life connection and by not knowing at the time we were together long ago on the other side. Once more he would be one of my spiritual teachers. He was guiding me and I would find this out much more in an amazing way!

Another message at that time came from an angel being of light has been: "The meek shall inherit the earth; thus it was written ages ago and so it remains true today. The journey is long but now the path has been lightened for you, and it is time to finish the book." This book I am writing now…

John would return letting me know he would stay close by to me for the next five days, and during that time in visions he did show me of past life-times. They were those we have spent together in England, Ireland, and also as American Indians. It was now becoming clearer to me the connections we all have, and how everything is all connected. It is he, John, who helped me write the poem Under the Rainbow Crossing that appears at the beginning of this book. He is thus another of my great teachers. I was overwhelmed with happiness.

Regarding my unsympathetic friends, the good ones in whom I have confided who simply did not understand what I was talking about; I have been shown in visions that they are shaking their heads behind my back. And thanks to the direction I encountered in the Bible passage and also from John at the psychic fair, I have since distanced myself from them not wanting to be seduced, as it were, by their misunderstanding. Also, not wanting to cause them any fear or make them feel uncomfortable it is certainly not my intention to promote these feelings! We all, after all, are on different journeys in life, and I'm sure mine is not for anyone but myself, just as other folk's journeys are only for them. I do try to stay open at all times to anything new. I tend to think that if we are not moving forward, we are then moving backward, and for me, life --- the feeling of being alive --- is ahead of me, not behind. If you keep looking behind one never moves forward.

Beverly once told me: "You will know whom to talk to. They'll know you and you will know them." We seem to somehow recognize one another when we are on a Universal spiritual level. In this way we can relate to each other and share experiences with one another. I feel it's like a circle, a network of us around the world, working, teaching, and learning for mankind and that's pretty much how it's been. I am grateful for the opportunities I have had to share these experiences with people who didn't cross themselves and suddenly disappear. There are many people who often have difficulty with the paranormal, and more often than that (it seems to me, anyway) forget all about compassion when they hear my stories.

Perhaps a general lesson we all are to learn during this earthly school-time is to face ourselves, to look in the mirror and to examine our own heart before we lash out and break another's. If people would only let go of guilt and fear and spend energy on fostering compassion and love, the world would be a much better place.

At this point I wish to thank a special relative of mine, Aunt Helen. I have always been able to confide in her since she has always been a wonderful listener and a great presence for me. She has been very patient and understanding when I have revealed my innermost thoughts and concerns. She has never disappointed me, and has been a source of great comfort for me during my journey of life changing events, into the less visible sides of life. I give my thanks to her and my eternal love.

Even when many of my friends disappointed me, however, I have found that the spirits often step in, consoling me during times of stress. This is a large part of my journey by learning to move on and keep on track. The spiritual beings life me up with words of love.

When I have encountered an upsetting situation, sometimes I would find a blue flower where one had not been a moment before! The first time I found a flower in this way I immediately looked around very quickly for someone who could have placed it there. Of course no one was to be found, or at least seen. After all, I was the only one in the house at the time this happened. I began to check the rooms and in a certain flower arrangement in the front parlor sure enough, a large blue flower was missing! I know that it is Katie who brings me the flower, just like a child, no? I marvel at the sweetness of this little spirit girl. How could I be afraid when our spirit friends are such dear friends? If my house is bad or evil, will someone please tell me what good is? If I were hearing and seeing terrible things that tried to harm and frighten us all, I would certainly know, and feel the overwhelming presence. If I were being told to do negative things I would certainly know.

This brings to mind a friend of mine in California who had many experiences in her home similar to some of these I am having in mine. After she risked telling a few of her friends about her strange encounters and wrote a book. She was labeled a witch, a cult member, and a Satanist (yes, even in California!) Due to cruel people she and her family felt compelled to sell their home and move away. I still can't believe how cruel some people can be, especially when all they have is ignorance of such matters. My Californian friend is very loving and a tolerant person, but the several small children she was raising at the time caused her to move in order to spare them any more unnecessary trauma. Fortunately, in their new location the family is doing well. Ignorance can do a world of harm to anyone…

Many times I think about how all of these new experiences I am having keep repeating lives, as though they comprise a circle of events. No real beginning, no real end, rather a circle, and my main spiritual guide began showing me a circle again and again. For a long time I was puzzled why a circle? I have since taken this image to point toward the constantly evolving nature of one's experience, at least when one is open to new things. How wonderful that my guide is here assisting me, prodding me, and challenging me. I know my guides to be Christ Light Beings that have chosen to re-enter time and space, but without fully leaving the other side. Sounds like a rather nice job, doesn't it? And it's all a matter of free will. They choose. We choose, everyone chooses, all the time. A guide can steer us in a certain direction, which is what I call the experience of being drawn, but we have the free will to decide to follow our intuition.

Sometimes I am drawn in such a manner during sleep; some people call this astral traveling as I do. I will leave my physical body in spiritual form and travel at incredible speeds, usually drifting toward wherever I need to go or see. During such episodes I will encounter spiritual beings in all corners of the vast universe. I feel as though I am but a tiny spark in a boundless space of current, of energy, pure energy, that is filled with personalities. I am always breathless with excitement on these light-speed journeys; I never want them to end. At times I am in the presence of our Universal Father, Christ, and I can feel his total and complete love and hear his words to me. There are no words in the earthly language to express this emotion. I want to stay in this magnificent beautiful place surrounded by this total love but know I cannot, I have much to do yet while I am here on earth.

Interestingly, the first time I was shown the universe in this fashion I wasn't sleeping, rather I videotaped it on our television set with the video camera using the television as a monitor only! I was directed by my spiritual teacher on how to do this since I have never done any of these procedures. The TV was now a monitor only. I focused the camera on different places in our middle parlor where the television is located, and when I swung the camera onto the television set the most shocking things appeared to be coming out of the set! There was my main spiritual teacher on the TV, not in the room, mind you to my eyes right then! Nevertheless there he was! His head was surrounded by white and golden light filling the screen. Then he nodded in my direction and began to move out of the set becoming a figure of beautiful light! The rest of the room seemed to disappear as I looked through the view finder and he would then fill the screen plainly visible upon play back on the television.

I was spellbound, needless to say and in fact moved to tears at the beauty, and the intimacy of it all. It was as if he was telling me that "what we all really are, down deep, is light and that even though each one of us may only be a spark in a vast current of energy, each of us is still very much a vital spark. A unique spark, a necessary spark: part of a whole and yet simultaneously and in fact constituted by the whole itself and this whole is itself constituted by love." Often when I videotape the room in this way there will be millions of gold and silver sparkles flying and spinning across the room sometimes in a man-made that is, not randomly designed vortex.

When I feel I am led to do so I set up the video camera still pointed toward the turned off television set, and walk over to stand in these points of gold and silver sparkles of light. I have been overwhelmed by

This is a picture from the amazing video that I have described on this page of my spiritual teacher Han Tai Chen Su moving out of the TV set and becoming a beautiful ball of light. You can plainly see his head and arms forming.

the love and warmth that I feel, it is beyond words. Then I receive my teachers' words: "See what the light is all about; see what love is all about; see what you are all about pass it on." Yes, I was learning how we are made of light, of energy, and to this day when I play back my videos at times, I still marvel at watching my spiritual teacher from the other side relate my lessons to me. At those times I always wish everyone could experience this great love and excitement. When Leon later viewed the videos that I recorded, he was absolutely spellbound, and later could not find words to speak, he only shook his head. I really believe he was near tears as I was.

I will always remember traveling in the night in astral travel around this same time frame, with one of my spiritual teachers for another of my lessons. He took me very high up into the universe so that I was looking down upon earth and all I could see was millions of pin- points of light everywhere in the darkness. I was told by him, "since we are all light, that's how the spirits see us from the other side and they are drawn to the lights." Now I knew how we looked then to the ones who have crossed over, and it was breathtakingly beautiful! Sometimes when I return very fast, it's like a person feels when one has fallen in a dream and you jump!

In the beginning when Beverly was visiting she began to receive a message from one of my guides, who wanted me to write it down. I got pen and paper and Beverly first asked me, "to write down this guides name, Han Tai Chen Su who seems to work with me most." I felt sure of this since he was teaching me so much and was a sage. He had been a philosopher in his earth life many, years ago, from when he lived in the Han Dynasty. He was very wise, and full of ancient wisdom. I was happy to know more about him and his life on earth. She then related his message which basically asked me to get a certain book at the library with hand in the title; and it would say published by Cambridge University Press. The cover of which would be colored in the same white and golden hues, as what I witnessed during my videotaping of him in the television set, these were my only clues to go on.

I was really anxious to get to the library the next day, but initially could not find the book in the areas of New Age or Psychic sections. Then I listened to my own thoughts and for that reason was drawn down the aisle to the American Indian section of books. This was an area such a book as I was told about would not normally be found. As I browsed in this Native American section a book suddenly fell out on top of my foot by itself! The cover of the book was colored with a golden and a white cover, in fact, published by Cambridge, and was titled The Handbook of Chinese Horoscopes! It looked to be an old book and had probably escaped the old book library sales several times. The book had to do with horoscopes and astrology, and for learning the different signs and meanings under the date of which people are born. One can learn about your own and others personalities, likes and quirks...

Since my study on horoscopes I have learned to not become attached to spiteful or hateful behavior the negative may demonstrate. This would be an important lesson for me from Han Tai Chen Su, in knowing how to bow and walk away. In other words, not let them take my energy. Perhaps they have not yet learned what free will is all about? Free will is one of my own most important lessons in this life, and because of what I read in this book I have become much better at

52

bowing before malicious behavior. Then by simply walking away I am untouched by the malevolent. I am very grateful for this small but very important book and my lessons in it. Hopefully, you can see how I began to learn many symbols, signs, and important ways, from my guides and teachers to get their messages across to me such as the clues to me on finding this important book. I felt absolutely *honored* by this grand introduction to Han Tai Chen Su, who would be with me every step of the way and throughout my life.

I was once told that in this line of work that some of us do, we need to think beyond a *psychiatrist*, in order to figure many things out. I was beginning to think that could be very possible. You are probably wondering why the messages come so many ways and I have no idea, other than to open different doors to me and teach me more focus. Later on I would receive many lessons concerning focus. I was told then my son and I was their Honorable students...

Now back to negative people who want to hurt us with words. Sometimes, however, words seem necessary to accompanying my bowing and walking away. At those times I ask my guides and teachers to give me something compassionate and constructive to say to people who would undermine my new found belief in myself. After all, meanness has to do with the person who is behaving in a mean fashion not in the object of meanness. When one bows and walks away, one is walking away from their problem, not one's own. I think this is what forgiveness is all about, though the term forgiveness notes an initial attachment to someone else's' problem, a taking of it personally, followed by a liberating detachment. Perhaps forgiveness, in a deeper sense can imply never being attached to malevolent in the first place, with manifesting or demonstrating free will in action in the face of those for whom free will is probably not very familiar. All I know for sure is that we all have free will, and that other people are in charge of theirs and I am in charge of mine.

Ultimately, while we are intimately interconnected with everything else, we are also constrained by our higher selves to not interfere with the lives of others. That is their task, not ours. Interference equals control, and control equals condemnation, and condemnation only inflates one's own suffering or unrest. To be on hand to help one is a good thing when we can, that is different than wanting to run another's life or needing to control another.

I learned all of this, or at least had much of it enforced upon me from the book at the library by the way of my teachers, guides and Beverly. It's as though we all have a predetermined background upon which our free will is, as it were, pitted. I guess the notion of free will would have never been formed if such were not the case: Free will notes a friction, an abrasion of sorts, and a challenge and becomes free will when it is freed, when it is realized, when one steps out from the background into which one has been put in too.

From the day at the library now knowing who this guide, Han Tai Chen Su was and had been in another time and space, I realized it was he alone who I was seeing in his colors on my television set. He had been trying to teach me many of my learning lessons, and was one of the faces in the magic mirror which hangs in our house. I also would find out later, he was my main guide, from the direction of the East, the same main direction as mine I was told.

This made everything more mysterious, like not knowing where and when this mirror that we nicknamed the magic mirror, arrived in our house and appeared on our wall! One day it was just there! We questioned everyone and no one knew about the mirror! We were all dumbfounded! This mirror would play a central role in the years and events to come. As time passed, I began to receive more communications from our new spirit friends residing in our home. A certain message came soon from the lumberjack who watches over us. He gave me a message to study a certain book, a volume owned by my son. He wanted me to remember the number 5, and he also spoke to me about my mother who was still a resident in the nursing home. He was another guardian to us and our home. I was learning why they were in my life now.

In one of our front bedrooms there is a tall chest with a lace scarf with some assorted pictures and figurines across the top of it. I began to notice that the scarf would be folded back very neatly towards one side of the chest. At first, I tried to think logically and that I had somehow folded it in a housekeeping frenzy. But when I would put the scarf back the way it used to be, when I returned back into the room I saw it again neatly and differently folded back! I knew that the *spirit* lady whom we have come to call the folding lady had been busy. Not only has she folded the same scarf on the chest over twenty times now, (I kept count) in addition she regularly has folded our washcloths, hand towels, pillowcases, dish towels, and other folding as well! I had an invisible housekeeper! She doesn't just fold things neatly in half or in quarters she is quite an artist. Her work displays intricate patterns and designs. When I lay something down, turn around, and look back it is already folded! One of the most beautiful things the folding lady did was with a chair that she wrapped.

I had gotten up early one day to leave for work and hurried downstairs to our bathroom to finish brushing my hair. Just before I entered the bathroom I looked over into our parlor and saw Leon's chair. I had placed a sheet over it the day before in order to protect it from the dust that he was creating during his remodeling. The sheet was now wrapped around the chair with the ends neatly tucked under the cushion, with part of the sheet around the back of the chair *braided* like a French braid of hair! Every stripe of the sheet lined up with perfection! I yelled out into thin air, "Oh my goodness!" Dropping my

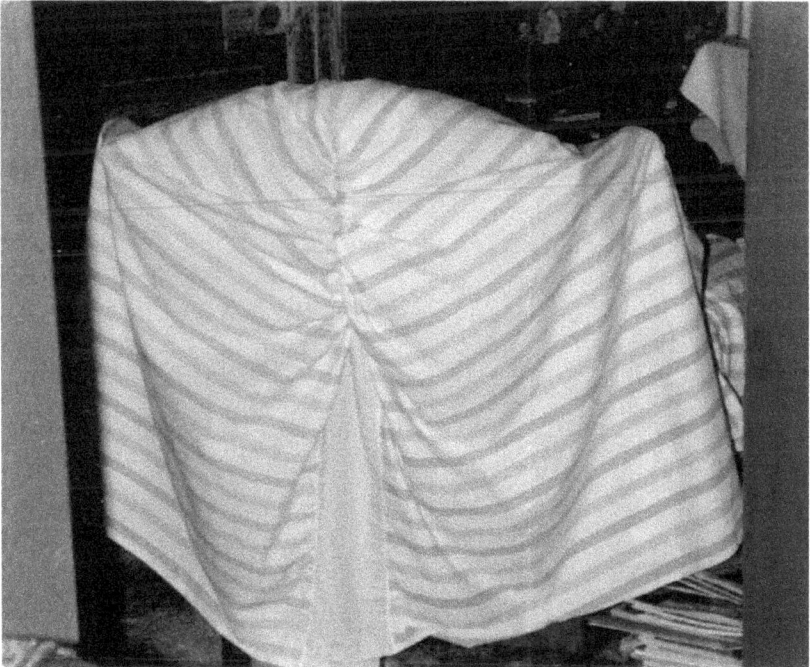

This picture is of a beautifully braided sheet that was created by the spirit we call the Folding Lady, who stays busy pleating and folding various items around the house.

brush I ran into the room and fell to my knees to get a closer look at the sheet art the folding lady had done. Gravity should have prevented such a creation from staying in place, but there it was, right in front of my eyes! I took some photographs quickly in case it fell away and called some family members over to see it. Close to approximately fourteen of us (family) viewed the sheet art and none of us could figure out exactly how it had been done! There was absolutely nothing to hold it together! That evening when Leon came home I excitedly showed him the creation on his chair.

Even though he was as dumbfounded about it, he wanted to sit down in his chair. We finally decided to undo the sheet so Leon could use his chair since we couldn't just sit and look at it forever. As soon as I gently touched the braided part it all fell away just as I felt it would. And secretly, I would like to have viewed the sheet art for at least another day to enjoy the beauty of it all and I was really happy that several others had gotten to view this event. And yes, I had lots of jokes thrown my way from my family about having a maid, with comments such as, "why don't you have her help with this and this." Unfortunately it doesn't work that way, I have no control over her cleaning habits and as much as it may seem to you these things really happened and continue to happen in our home.

Pictures move around to different places, upstairs and down, our coffee machine will turn off and on its own, doors open and close, lock and unlock, bottles are opened, and figurines turn up in other rooms and different footprints are seen here and there. One holiday while cooking several loaves of bread were found placed end to end on the floor as if some child (Katie) wanted them to look like a train.

Remember when Chris blessed the spirits so they could go into the light if they wanted too? That's why my conclusion is, I have no doubt they have the same free will we have all been given. I know that is how they continue to move back and forth as they wish. To come and go to live again in their time doing their regular things as they did in their lives here on earth, or go over into the other side if they wish.

A while back my son sent me a pink quartz rock in the mail as a gift and it disappeared the same day that it arrived! Several weeks passed and he came home for a visit. I apologized for not having the rock, explaining how it had quickly disappeared. David said, "Don't worry, mom; it'll probably be back soon --- perhaps someone needed it for a reason, who knows." That's the way we look at these things.

The next night as we were watching television David had that strange faraway look he gets when he is hearing a message coming through. He was staring vacantly into the room as he said, "I know where the rock is now!"

I replied, "Where do you see it?"

'It's in the little front bedroom upstairs on my communion plate!"

This bedroom is never used though I had cleaned it just prior to his arrival in order to freshen it. I knew the rock had NOT been there. We ran up the stairs into the bedroom and there it was right where he said it would be! So my rock was returned after all and I felt there was a strong message to both of us by it being centered onto the communion plate and being a holy object. This would not end up being the only time my rock disappears which is another story. Objects continued to come and go around here. We just figure there is always a reason that we don't have to understand or know; maybe later it will make sense. Right now my scissors are missing and a beautiful little statue, I trust they will be back but if not perhaps they are needed someplace else, who knows?

One day I planned to use two antique lamp shades for a light fixture we had recently purchased. I had stored them on Leon's workbench until we needed them. When the light was installed and we were ready to use them I went to the workbench and they were gone! We looked everywhere for them but in vain. Again, only the two of us live in this house so there was no possibility of children mischievously moving or hiding them. I called David to get any information intuitively and I asked if he could see them; he told me he did, "They were in the old barn wrapped in paper!" Upon visiting the barn Leon and I found them just where he said they would be wrapped in old newspaper! The shades had previously been in the garage! Your guess is as good as mine regarding just how the spirits transport these solid objects.

Continuing with moved objects my reading glasses are often moved. Upon taking a picture of them, when I find them there invariably is a haze around them, and with other items that have been moved. I feel this is some kind of energy residue from a spirit friend who did this. Once there appeared in my bedroom a tiny white footprint in the mauve carpet beside the bed stand! I am sure this small footprint belonged to Katie. Who knows how or why, but it's in the photograph I took as plain as day. I had realized early on she likes to play jokes the same as any five year old child normally does.

Another fascinating experience took me completely by surprise one day while upstairs. This was an editing of a recording I wanted to keep. This recording is also very dear to me, and was made on a reel-to-reel audiotape of one of my little granddaughters. She was three years old singing her favorite song, "I Just Called to Say I love you." I made this tape sometime ago and I got to thinking about it that particular day, and played it again for old time's sake. To my great surprise after the first normal playing of her little voice the song started up again, but this time her voice had changed greatly and was accompanied by a number of backup singers!

Some of the voices were obviously male and some were female. The one female had an extremely southern voice and one was badly off key, unbelievable but true! I made copies onto a cassette player I had around the house and thanked the spirits for their song to me then I asked them if they would put my granddaughters' voice back on the original way since I only had the one copy. Around that time Leon came home and I couldn't wait to tell him what had happened. After he sat down I played the song for him and the spirits version was still on the reel to reel. I thought he was going to pass out by the way his face looked! He left quickly shaking his head.

Early the next day I played the song to see if it was back to normal, and sure enough all traces of the edited version was gone! In its place was my granddaughter's voice back on it singing her song! I played the cassette of the spirit voices singing for our family I loved it so much! I knew the meaning of the message that they were sending to us, that they do love us and are truly happy. Every once in awhile I get out the cassette tape and play the spirits version and we truly believe they were singing of their love for us. This seemed to make a good imprint on Leon after he settled down and he was more content now.

As I have said, the spirits are apparently very fond of us. When I would run the vacuum sweeper sometimes the cord would actually move by itself on the floor into the shape of a heart! At other times it would actually rise up off of the floor maintaining its heart shape! I have very clear pictures of the sweeper cord in this way.

This began to happen around that time with the lamp cords, they would do the same thing. The lamps would at times turn on and off and so would the sweeper by themselves, even though no one was using either one at least by no one we could see at the time that is! It was as if we were playing some sort of game so perhaps Katie Jane was just having some fun. I would unplug the sweeper and the cord would keep changing into the *heart shape* with it turned off, so it really didn't matter if it was plugged in or not. Whoever caused this the message is clear: the *heart* shape has to do with my parent's family name... and another thing I know is that our house is full of love and I do love to pursue our friends as they seem to pursue us.

These experiences seem to be for me in order to learn what the spirits can do with the funny jokes they play to show their humor. No matter what film and camera I use the spirits here virtually always edit the finished product. I welcome any professional photographer or scientific laboratory to examine these photographs. I certainly have nothing to do with how they appear. For my part I can hardly take a picture of a group of people without chopping their heads off.

In the downstairs bathroom the spirits will choose certain things to move around for a period of time. Sometimes they move items back and forth and at other times they will continually choose new locations for them. I can't say for sure whether they are just moving around in their own dimensions or whether they are just reminding me of their presence. Perhaps their object moving is like a game for them. We have a certain soap dish in the shape of an angel that would often move around on the vanity. I would take pictures of it in the various places to which it moved, and did my best to take pictures of it while it was moving if I was lucky. Some of these pictures show blurry speed lines around the perimeter of the dish to mark its movement. This is as an object will look when it is moving at a terrific speed.

My son David has a large old silver cross on a stand which was used at one time in a church somewhere along time ago. Every once in a while we find this cross has turned and each time faces the east! The first time it did this I was actually standing beside it, and upon seeing it turn wondered what was being communicated!

In meditation with the cross I was told again "my main direction is the east" how important this must be I thought to myself. I would keep this memory in my mind from then on.

One morning about 5:00 am I heard a loud crash and immediately arose to investigate. The old cross had fallen onto the bedroom floor and we were leaving on a trip that day. I wondered if someone was trying to tell us not to go. We went on our trip anyway and I asked for a confirmation that we would be alright. I then received my answer in the way I get my information from the other side. I was told I would see a huge cloud formation of a big cross in the sky as we traveled. By this sign I knew we would be perfectly safe. Sure enough, about one hour away on the highway I looked up to see just that! There in the sky was a cloud formation of a huge cross that followed us along for many miles that day! Perhaps the lesson in this event was to believe more in myself and to also have more faith in the words and visions I was getting to trust more in my new work.

Generally speaking, most of the photographs I take in the house portray parts of it looking wavy and soft (dimensional.) The colors are almost always tinted in a way that looks quite different to the naked eye my children called it dreamy looking. Our home just doesn't look real either. I have one picture of the front parlor that blows the mind; it is all in strange dimensions and colors. When looking at a picture of our large mirror over the fireplace when it's inside the same mirror is a shock! It is one of my favorites! In another picture I took the same day you can plainly see some of the furniture through other furniture, and two of some things and one of others in dimensions!

At Christmas, our tree with its decorative lights doesn't look real either in pictures. Christmas time around here is really exciting the spirits are really busy! They do all kinds of lovely things, even to place items under the tree! The funny part is these items come from somewhere else in the house! It is as if they want to be a part of the decorating of the tree and rooms. They will at times move the nut crackers about and once they lined up all the nutcrackers on the staircase as if they were marching down the stairs! Just like Charley did one Christmas…

Another funny thing at Christmas was when a man's watch, which came up missing, was placed onto the wrist of a large toy Santa that we had standing beside the front door! Sometimes we laugh until we are exhausted. It seems to David and me the spirits are entertaining us… The outside photographs are very different and beautiful, that is, they seem to be edited in another time. Snowflakes will appear bigger than life and look cloud like. In one photo I could see a man's face inside of one! Often in the pictures there will be a white fog over the top of the house and across the yard. In reality in front of the house there is not a real fog anywhere! I can't take a picture outside of our house without the night sky full of orbs everywhere and spirit lights in front of our home, which is beautiful!

When our daughter Lynn was growing up we arrived home and was parking in the driveway after being out for the evening. Lynn said, "She saw three large balls of light over our house lighting up the sky." At that time I was still a tiny bit of a *skeptic* about such matters due to her being a child. Whether or not my cynicism prevented me from seeing them I don't know, but now I see in my own photographs the same similar phenomena.

Working in the yard when I look up at the windows from outside I can sometimes see faces in the glass or somewhere near the glass. Someone likes to watch, a little girl, a woman, a man, or other spirits. As I documented on film the remodeling we are doing to the exterior of the house, my pictures are regularly tinted with balls or other shapes of soft light around the house and shrubs. These orbs are in blue, orchid, pink, green, gold and white in color, floating throughout the yard.

We have laughed about the place that develops my film, wondering if they have time to notice my strange pictures. Since I have been very private about all of this I change places quite frequently when I drop off my film. I did have one incident where the developer said, "My pictures were lost." These pictures had some of my guides and other dimensional objects in them. I knew someone there had seen them and wanted to keep the pictures. With help from Beverly I knew just the right words to say and in two hours I had my pictures back! The pictures were *suddenly* found after I called back and let the right words be said, that I was directed to say.

When I video an old stained glass church window that we have and not touching the controls on the camera, when we play back the tape the room begins to glow. Suddenly there would be a huge ball of golden light which moves from the window to right in front of me and the camera. I know who this is now. I could hold out my hand and actually feel the warmth and intelligence of this spiritual being. The ball at times change in shape and colors shining through my fingers just like an aura. Once I put the video camera on a table as this was happening and stepped into this golden ball of light, the love I felt from it nearly moved me to tears. I cannot find words to begin to describe the feelings of this blessed moment. My tapes are filled with such things. I would be absolutely stunned with all of this beauty and thinking to myself how amazing my life is filled with these secrets I could not speak of...

Around the date of my late mother's birthday last year something told me to start my video camera. I often get inspired in such a fashion by my spiritual teachers. I soon had the camera ready and started taping the parlor (remember that I have disconnected the television from my cable line in order to use it as a monitor only.) First I noticed a soft blue and brilliant white color beginning to form at one edge of my mother's picture I have on the wall. While I taped the colors on her picture would first move slowly across it as if through her hair and turn her hair to a bluish white shade! Then the colors began to take shapes, beside her face appeared a woman and a babies face! Quickly the colors formed another small child's face and then an infant! I was so excited I was ecstatic, watching the colors fade in and out as the camera focused! I could NOT believe what was happening!

After this happened there was more to come! A beautiful ball like object in shimmering layers of gold's and blues floated up to the left side of her picture where it situated itself in front of my mothers' picture. All the while I was trying to tape with one eye looking into the camera with what was happening and looking into the room with my other eye. I saw the objects with both eyes, and I prayed that the tape was recording what I was seeing. Please let this be on tape! Thinking back all of a sudden, I remembered reading about Shape Shifters and thought of my Indian Shaman guide. This made me realize how my mother and I had the same Shaman who my sons' too. I prayed all of what I was recording would be on the tape. When I looked it over after it faded away everything was perfectly recorded! I have it all on tape! What a birthday gift from my mother and spiritual teacher.

I am simply not the same person that I was just a few years ago thanks to my spiritual beings and the Big Picture, with which they have blessed me. Later on, when my pictures were developed I could plainly see the Beings on mother's picture and the profile of my Shaman in his beautiful layers of gold and blues. My main guide the Shaman teacher, and my mother were certainly expressing some important lessons in my teachings. I took the one small child in the picture to be none other than Katie Jane, and perhaps some of the other spirits who are here. I have not been told yet who they all are.

Waking up in the morning is exciting! I wonder what I will learn that day and going to sleep is exciting as well---I wonder what I will learn from my dream states. I keep a journal making sure to write down all my experiences to make the most of them. In addition to dreaming I found I was able to focus more on astral traveling at night in order to move through the universe. During these times I felt at one with everything and every place and at times I am fully awake.

When this travel happens I can feel my spirit self take off with a tremendous movement of speed, knowing I have left earth and am out of my body and in my energy form. The feeling I get tends to be filled with joy though other times are like dreams, and others seem to be the product of a luminal state of consciousness in which I am betwixt and between wakefulness and sleep, yet very lucidly aware of the experience. I'm sure some people have heard stories on this subject by those who have been out of body during surgery and other times. This is sometimes called an NDE (near death experience.) Usually those who remember their experience begin a new journey in their life afterwards. Their life changes dramatically for the good. There are many mysterious ways we can learn from that one may never have thought about as possible.

My brother Teddy is truly the world's greatest skeptic with regard to spirits and other paranormal phenomena as I mentioned earlier. He arrived one day and brought his own video camera over to the house to discover whether we would both get the same results. He wanted us to simultaneously tape the same things at the same time. I had been telling him about the extraordinary events in the middle parlor with our mothers' picture. We spent about a half hour or so taping and he noticed his camera seemed to have had a mind of its own! It did what it wanted without his assistance! When he finally got exasperated enough he said, "if this thing does anything else out of the ordinary I'm going home!" He then attempted to rewind the tape in preparation for playing it discovering it had already rewound itself! He sat his camera down on a nearby table as soon as he recovered from the rewinding surprise. Then he went to take out the tape from the camera and noticed it had fast-forwarded itself to the end again! His camera continued to do all sorts of things by itself so without another word he picked up his camera and said, "I'm going home!" He left muttering to himself and shaking his head. At the door of his car he shouted out, "I would be finding me a new place to live!" In conclusion to that visit I believe my brother had an experience he will always remember.

Beverly came over in a few days and I showed her the tape of the lights and shapes around my mothers' photograph in the parlor. She paused a few moments then said, "He is your Shaman." This observation she gave me sealed my second confirmation. I could clearly make out his profile in the glimmering layers of gold and blue. She had sensed the Shaman and wondered whether the Shaman was one of our ancestors and now she knew he was.

There is another striking and extraordinary event of when these photographs were developed. On two of my mother's pictures on her throat is the red Sacred heart of Jesus! I would begin to find more new pictures I took of her with this red heart shape on her throat as well. What, it all means I cannot say at this time, for the information has not been given to me as yet and perhaps never will. But I will say that this event has made me extremely humble to put it mildly. I know one thing her spiritual work was very important when she was here on earth and still now that she is in her Heaven.

My mother's picture with layers of blue and white light that would begin forming through her hair. When I was filming this the sacred heart appeared on her throat.

Months later on my mother's birthday once again, I was to be witness to the sign of the Sacred Heart of Jesus once more! I entered

64

the bathroom to prepare for the day and I stopped in my tracks! My mothers' picture the same 5x7 had been removed from the wall, was standing upright and was sitting on the counter! A scarf was over the top of the picture like a head covering in Bible times! I have no words to give it a true description! I was in complete awe…all I could do is to feel very blessed and humble! I confess I couldn't get myself together for several moments. I then took pictures and waited for a message to come. This told me she was on a high level. All week I could think of nothing else.

I have no explanation to all of the correct meaning. I am sure this told me of where she was doing her spiritual work. All I did know is that there was something so wonderful going on in my life and the answers would all come in time.

On another visit to our son David, I had an interesting astral experience the first night we slept in his home. Upon going to bed I hardly closed my eyes and the next thing I remember is making my way back to our house miles away in spirit. I was suddenly in bed lying on my right side looking out into the spare bedroom. I quickly saw a male spirit figure come into my room from the window. He was going around my side of the bed from where he could be unseen, someplace behind me! I could feel his *evil* presence immediately along with a *threatening* cold breeze behind my head and against the back of my neck! I knew he was not there for benevolent reasons! He wanted to terrify me!

I knew in my heart I needed to call for my Angels, Protectors, and the Heavenly Father. I also wondered where our guardian lumberjack was at that moment, I needed help! Simultaneously, I realized that *evil* feed off of our *fear* so I calmly called out to my protectors, and I immediately felt his presence fade from me and he was gone! This evil presence had apparently traveled through a dimension right into our house! I felt the spirits here were in frenzy; they certainly did not want any kind of evil presence in this house!

The next morning I asked my son if he had any unusual dream states the night before. He said, "Don't you remember?" It was as though he expected me to know that we had shared this astral experience. I was shocked that he was there! I told him, "I didn't know he and the lumberjack was with me the night before!" He related the entire experience to me and spoke of how this evil thing was trying to terrify me in the bedroom back at our home. And how the lumberjack and he had also helped to get rid of the intruder! I believe that in addition to the help of the Holy ones, David, and the lumberjack is what allowed me to escape unscathed from the intruder, was also my conscious effort to first realize my fear, and then quickly bring it under control. After all, I had been taught about different types of fear from my spiritual family for some time now. Perhaps what is known as possession occurs when fear is not conquered; I definitely believe it is fear that invites negativity towards oneself.

I have to think that such control, such free will, is especially important for us in our haunted house where apparently both benevolent and occasionally a malevolent presence has somehow entered through. Thankfully the malevolent cases have been almost non-existent in our home. I am thankful for our protection in these matters. This kind of experience can and does happen over our world.

I take many house pictures of each experience to record the amazing things which happen here. There are times I find a picture included with mine I didn't take! It amazes me when I pick up my photos and find a picture I did not take or have any knowledge of! The spirits apparently take pictures with their energy with my camera!

David had given me a large beautiful crystal ball one day as a gift. It had belonged to an elderly woman who in her lifetime was a psychic. The ball was at least 100 years old! It had been stored with her belongings 25 years prior to her death and was from a sale from her estate years after her death. When I picked up my developed pictures did I get big surprise! I could tell one photo was of my bedroom (by the fireplace.) In the photo my crystal ball appears to be floating through the air almost to the ceiling! It seems to be full of energy and sparkling lights with a greenish and dazzling brilliant white glow, it is normally clear. This is a favorite picture of mine…We still can't begin to explain this! This is a very solid and heavy ball.

Another thing that the experiences in our house have led me to absolutely believe for some time, is that at our core we are not matter but all energy. Fear is one kind of energy and compassion is another kind. There are a zillion types of energy everywhere. We have all heard about bad vibes being omitted from a person or in a place. Bad vibes are fear vibes and are felt, I think, by the psychological agent known as intuition. Fear can be confronted and overcome by compassion, by not attaching yourself to the fear, and by not allowing it to become attached to you. Their fear is not your fear or it doesn't have to be to be sure. While strong words are perhaps sometimes necessary to counter the fear that is dictating the condemnatory behavior of others. I have found that if you condition yourself to not let their fear touch you, your positive energy will either embarrass or frustrate the malevolent fearful person. It may even make them realize that they are completely out of control, enough that, they may learn something positive from their behavior to help themselves change a few things to the positive.

CHAPTER THREE
Seeing the Spiritual Forms

In our home is what we call a Magic mirror. It hangs on the wall over the staircase at the top of the stairs to our bedroom. This is the mirror that none of us know where it could possibly have come from, and has always been a mystery! We can remember with unusual precision where the rest of our furniture came from but the mirror has no identity of its own. The mirror experience began one day when I was walking down the staircase and for some reason I felt to turn around. I was compelled to look back up the stairs, and for a moment I doubted my sanity! Placed on the wall over the landing was an old mirror I had never seen before! All I could ask myself was, "where did THAT come from, am I really seeing a mirror!" The events going on here in the house daily already more than amazed me! In the strange mirror I could swear I saw faces staring back at me! Did Leon somehow bring this old mirror home and hang it up? I doubted he did and not tell me, as we discussed all of our buying. Besides the mirror was at least 4 feet tall and I could also faintly see faces! I couldn't have missed seeing it!

Relax, I thought, go to the kitchen and get some window cleaner and clean the mirror you'll feel normal again, I hoped! With that silly thought I know I was upset! The cleaner did not remove the faces I could see however, no matter how hard I scrubbed. A few moments later I began to notice something in the mirror looked familiar, as I looked closer there were not just one or two faces, but three men's faces! One face familiar to me was Uncle Leo and one was John, one of the owners of this home long ago. The 3rd face was my Eastern teacher and guide Han Tai Chen Su. Clearly there were three of my teachers looking back at me!

The Magic mirror shown here is in a dimensional form. The camera captured three entities, (lower left) which appear to be ready to re-enter the portal. The portal is shown by the fine white lines in the mirror.

John was a nick name for one of the owners long ago. I watched the mirror off and on until Leon came home I was so traumatized!

He found me at the door babbling about a mirror that had appeared! I found out Leon knew NOTHING about this mirror and went to see it for himself. I strongly believe that mirrors are some way thresholds to other dimensions, to other places, that were also created. We tend to think we were the only living beings created and that earth has the only life. I believe that is a huge myth especially to what I have experienced by now. We have a vast universe full of other universes and worlds.

I can only share what has been given to me. I feel our universal Father created much more than we could ever perceive. I can only relate my experiences to you, the readers. In addition to the faces in the mirror that I continue to see peering back at me from over the staircase, I also see balls of light floating in and out of the mirror most times. I still don't believe I had fully realized my ability to see into all kind of phenomenon and strange things. I wasted no time getting my camera out and I began to video the mirror and have recorded all three faces there. I will never let this mirror leave our house it is important to me.

My deceased uncle, the one in the mirror taught and studied parapsychology, and was thus not unacquainted in his lifetime with encounters of many kinds. Perhaps the kind I am relating to you in this book. I did not know this about him until after he had passed away to the hereafter. He had lived away from this location most of his lifetime. I would of liked to shared all of this with him.

In any event I feel several of our loved ones, spirit teachers, guides and angels all together are watching out for us here, and are helping in many ways with our journey. When I tape these gentlemen in the mirror I can at times see their mouths moving but cannot seem to pick up on what they are telling me. I must say I never pass by that mirror that their presence is not in it to me. I feel that they are encouraging me along the path I am taking now and providing a very comforting peacefulness for me. I was sure by now Leon was deep into thought of what would all of this come to with the new changes in our life with the other side. He was still upset about the everyday events that he was stuck with for now. While I, on the other hand felt so very blessed to be given this gift of learning. I was able to understand how important this all was whether it was made clear now or whenever. I just knew it was and I trusted because I believe in the Fathers promise to all of us here on earth. This was a phenomenal and great spiritual awaking for me.

At times passing the mirror I would see gold light shoot out of Uncle Leo's eyes! On one occasion in a picture I took of Uncle Leo, once again appeared the sacred heart of Jesus appearing on his brow! Just like on my mother's picture, though hers always appeared on her throat! I know this is not a coincidence and there was quite a time factor in between the two events happening.

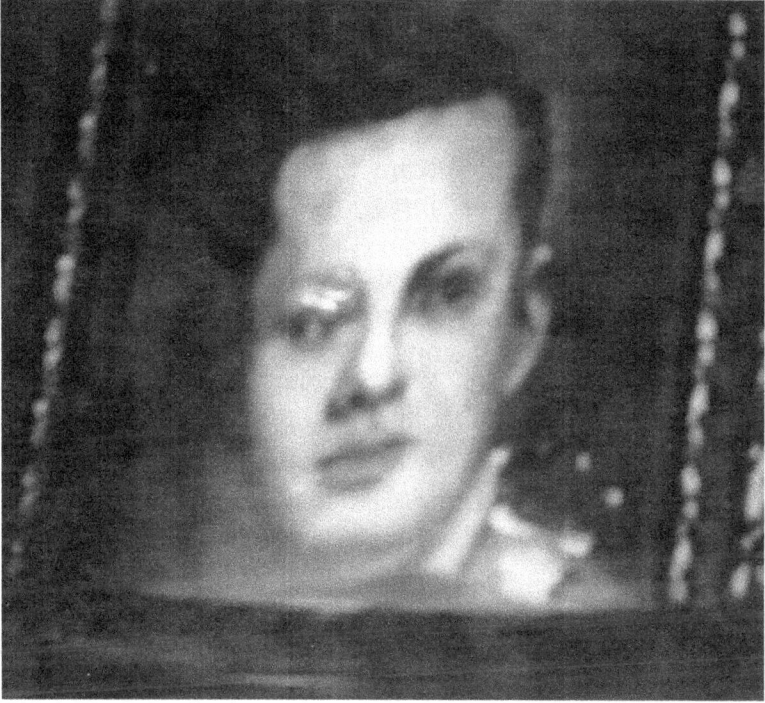

This is Uncle Leo's picture in a dimensional form showing the sacred heart that mysteriously appeared on his brow. This occurred at a separate time than when the sacred heart appeared in my mother's picture.

Sometimes when I have looked into the mirror I see two reflections of myself, one normal and one rather translucent. The translucent reflection will move around the solid reflection indicating that I am spiritual energy that is located by a material body. But to see *two* of yourself in a flat, unbroken mirror is fascinating to say the least! One particular time I looked into the magic mirror and suddenly I could see a man starring back at me! We scared each other so badly we both actually jumped! I could tell by his shocked expression he couldn't believe what he was seeing as well! I am sure we somehow entered one another's dimension since they overlap. He was dressed as in the 1800' with a curled up at the corner moustache, and wearing a tall black hat.

This was an experience I bet he will never forget as well as me! I watched for him off and on a few times but it never happened again.

The second time I saw a spiritual self I was taken by complete surprise. Since it was not my own self that I saw, and since no mirror was involved, I have to admit that the experience did startle me. It also made me more curious to search more.

This rare experience was on a summer day when I climbed up the ladder that was leaning against the house. It was leading to the roof where my husband was working. As I arrived at the top of the ladder I saw the figure of another man over my husband! The man appeared to be transparent and was hovering just above him, I froze in place! The apparition had the same build and size as Leon and I could see right through it to the trees and sky beyond. When Leon finished what he was doing in that spot and began to walk across the porch roof to the other side the form seemed to jump down in front of him, as if to lead the way! I noticed that Leon had a baseball cap on and as I slowly forced myself to look at the apparition's head so did it! It was at that moment I knew that the form must be some reflection of Leon. It was Leon! It must of been a kind of spiritual doppelganger, some alter ego.

I scrambled down the ladder as quickly as I could before I fell off. Leon had not noticed I was even there. Was the spiritual presence a bad sign or a good sign? Was something going to happen to him? My feet hit the ground running to the phone that is, and I called Beverly. She must have thought I was only babbling at first. Finally, I let her respond to my barrage of questions. She explained, "That I had seen his other self which was a very rare occurrence that most others cannot see. The apparition did not mean that anything was going to happen to him she assured me and, that I had merely witnessed a physical overlapping between Leon's spiritual body and his physical form. Because of the period in my life and perhaps the light of day as well, things were right for actually seeing that which under normal circumstances cannot be seen! We all slip in and out of our bodies all the time, when we dream and do astral traveling for instance.

Her comforting words did a lot to calm me down and since that time I have continued to see my own spiritual self several times. I regard any and all such phenomena as gifts, whether or not I know how to interpret them and I am extremely grateful for being exposed to them, Wow, what a day that was!

One day around 2:00 pm I was lying on the sofa trying to take a nap. I happened to glance at a beam across our ceiling and noticed a small black wheel- like form adjacent to the beam. The object was round like a ball but had the appearance of a saw-blade, the kind with jagged edges all the way around it. The circle also had a bit of orange coloring on it and slowly as I was watching it began to roll along the ceiling from one beam to another, whereupon it simply vanished! Needless to say, again I was up and running to the telephone and immediately called Beverly.

As I described what I saw she said, "She was able to mentally picture the black wheel, and explained that it probably was a being of light that lives in my house that perhaps has a reason to speak to me. She had never seen such a wheel herself, but had heard of others who have and a man's hand was turning the wheel, but she could pick up no more on the phenomenon."

While we were talking on the phone I asked her to tell me more about the folding lady. She paused for another moment, "The folding lady's dress was mauve in color and made from a cotton or cotton-like material. Black buttons made their way down the front of the dress in the shape of a V the point of which arrived at the waist." As she described the clothing I could picture it in my mind, and several times I anticipated her description, which made me feel good. Perhaps, I was sharpening my own clairvoyant skills. I imagined the folding lady's hair to be coal black and pulled back behind her head. Later as I was videotaping my bedroom all of a sudden right in front of my camera I saw part of a mauve dress with the same v at the waist with black buttons, walk by quickly! I pulled the camera away from my face to see but she had vanished!

As I rested on another afternoon a few days later, I suddenly heard a male's deep voice at the end of the sofa. I heard him speak three words very audibly, but I couldn't quite make them out. Perhaps the voice belonged to the man who turned the wheel and he was still trying to make contact with me. I hoped he would make another attempt to tell me his message.

The folding continued, my gloves and car keys would be moved to different places, footsteps in all the rooms became increasingly visible and even audible. Sometimes the foot prints would indicate a man's shoe, sometimes a woman's and at other times they appeared to be bare feet. None of the prints were in our size and Katie Jane's foot is so small I knew immediately who they belonged to, and many times her prints indicate that she goes without shoes.

One funny joke played on me was when I would find my gloves filled out as if my fingers was still inside of them, and bent in all sort of directions! Even the wrist opening would be filled out! This went on all winter each time I took my winter gloves off. And sometimes my car keys were standing up with every key on end by themselves! The spirits here certainly loved to make me laugh. It is sort of a strange feeling to be witness to these events, not scary, just strange, to know we all are living here, but in other dimensions. Again for me this makes it clear that life after life exists without any doubt. The spirits were positive and seemed to be reliving theirs.

Soon I needed to file some records into a correct order. I was at the library table (the spirit school teachers desk) making a new set of index files for my paranormal records. When I reached the U section I paused, hoping I had bought enough blank folders so I could make a duplicate set of files to Z. Upon looking back at my work I saw that I had a duplicate set of folders, which wasn't there a moment before! Just like I had been thinking! I called my son over to take a look since he was only a few feet away it was then I knew our resident schoolteacher had assisted me and could duplicate my handwriting at will! I now had enough folders somehow! I again experienced this duplication and phenomenon one day as I wrote checks to pay bills. All of a sudden instead of having one written check per bill I had two, which was in the same handwriting as mine! This must have happened in the blink of an eye (stopping time) because I hadn't paused to think or day dream and I wouldn't be doubling my checks! The only explanation I can find has to do with how time means nothing to the spirits on the other side. I haven't a clue why she decided I needed two checks per bill, but perhaps she was only helping me. We laughed about how we had better watch her check writing!

I realize the spirits must have a way to make our time stand still without our knowledge, for them to do things like this. Then we are back doing our jobs not even realizing what really happened. After she had finished her check writing that day I suddenly heard the door beside me open and close, with no one I could see. I figured she left to go back to wherever she goes, perhaps to the other side or to another duty. Who knows?

One day very early I was in our bathroom getting ready to go to work and I heard Leon call out, "What?" as though he was asking me a question to be repeated. I opened the door and asked him what he wanted.

He replied, "What do you want?" I told him I had been washing my face and trying to wake up. He got a funny look on his face and said, "Someone had clearly called out his name twice!" I told him it hadn't been me! He was fairly shaken at physically hearing a spiritual ladies voice that sounded like mine! One of the extraordinary things about Leon hearing voices at any time is that he has endured a great hearing loss, and it is difficult for him to hear well most of the time. It seems to us that the spirit world can certainly get through to whomever they wish too and this is what really startled Leon!

One evening he dared to turn in early leaving me down stairs watching television, as he stepped into our bedroom he could see two of the men spirits face to face! They seem to be having a conversation by the closet door! He quickly exited into the bathroom for awhile where he could hear the voices but could not make out the words. Many times I would hear them also, for some reason the words were usually muffled and I am surprised Leon wasn't close to a break down!

When I get spirit messages that I pick up mentally, on some occasions they are very clear and as loud as any person speaking. Perhaps it depends on whom and where they are coming from, I don't know. A few months later after Leon experienced the two males by the closet door; I too, had a one to one encounter. I rushed out of the bathroom one night turning off the light as I closed the door. I stopped suddenly saying, "Oh, I'm sorry Leon I didn't see you there in the dark." I had sort of bumped into what I thought was Leon but when I slid into bed I found him sleeping soundly! I knew then I had run into a *solid* form!

Another experience was when I turned into bed early one night. A little later I noticed Leon walking by my side of the bed going into the bathroom. He left the door ajar about six inches which was very unusual. I couldn't sleep because of the light filtering into the bedroom. I waited a long time for him to come out and go to bed then I began to be concerned after awhile so I walked over to the door and called out to him and received no answer. I slowly pushed back the door the rest of the way only to find an empty room! About that time he came upstairs and I told him what had happened. He had been downstairs the entire evening! Sometimes the spirits are solid when I see them, it's amazing!

By now the voices were becoming more clear, filled with transcendent messages of light and love, assuring me that I was moving along the right path, and that I was right on track.

One of the beautiful heavenly messages I received was, "Come, let me show you the way" and was particularly meaningful and uplifted me. I trust that our teachers and guides will not give us more than we can handle and I have promised myself to keep moving inward, toward myself: I think that direction comes first, so that by balancing and healing anything within us that needs balancing and healing we may be freed to be of assistance to others. In my experience, balancing and healing come by way of release. We become whole by letting things go, and I take great comfort in the spiritual help that we have along the way.

Along with my spiritual teachers and guides I have found reading to be very valuable. It has been so important for me to expose myself to both ancient wisdom, literature, and more contemporary philosophies.

This was also important in my healing work in many concepts. Some people may heal by their touch, and others may heal by their words, it's all out there for those who are looking and searching. It all has to do with learning how to release the old, in order to make way for the new. It has to do with letting go of the Little Picture, which eats away at us by their temptations toward negativity and fear, so with knowledge of the Big Picture, the condemnatory posturing of others can be much more easily ignored.

More spirit visits arrived wherever I went, they can appear anywhere. One day when I was visiting my Aunt Helen I was chatting with her as she sat on the sofa I saw a male figure appear beside her. He was outlined in gold and was very tall and seemed very familiar to me. As I focused more I recognized my father, Aunt Helen's brother. It was hard for me to keep my attention focused to her and talking with dad standing right beside her, but I tried to do so because I didn't want to frighten her. My father as well as others appears to me quite frequently, both when I am with other people and when I am alone and it is rather hard to follow conversations when I am with others, since I may be getting information from the other side at the same time. It's doing two things at one time in two different worlds which takes intense concentration.

It has taken a lot of practice for me to not show what Leon calls my "out there" expression on my face. Perhaps one day I will be able to keep a more normal look. By the way, later on, I was able to tell my Aunt about dad's visit that day and she was very receptive and happy about it, even with her teachings of a strict religion of fear.

I began to notice my photographs would sometimes change *after* the film had been developed! This was really a shocker! Some photos would include my son's furniture in them, even though he lived hundreds of miles away at the time! The furniture would be situated with some of the pieces sideways, and some upside down and disproportionate in size. In some of the pictures not only was my son's furniture mingled with mine, but some of the rooms in my house were see through along with some furniture solid and in dimensions.! For instance, the ceiling fans might be on the side of a wall and so on! David's bathroom vanity at his home would be located in my family room in my pictures! They are extremely interesting to view. The both of us were quite amazed to put it mildly. In the beginning for some time I was being taught about dimensions and now things added up! A good three years were mainly devoted to learning about dimensions. The other side worked with us with love.

I soon received a message from the Christ light Beings reinforcing that, "Things are not as they seem." I have certainly related it to the many unusual experiences I have had in our house the last few years. But mainly the meaning meant how I believed my old ways before the Heavenly Beings of Light came forth to teach me. I was then told to, "Leave the old ways behind" and I did I have never looked back! We are led to believe so many manmade ideas with how we are conditioned, generation after generation. But now, I have my spiritual teachers showing me the other worlds, universes, and how we live in an Illusion world on Earth.

In their worlds my son and I was their pupils and they worked with us to sharpen the intuitive senses. The Light Beings messages helped me with more insight to others, and to know we each are much more than we can ever imagine! With my son being a spiritual teacher to me in his life and the other Beings of Light I knew I had the best teachers I could have. My son being an old soul was waiting for me to remember.

One afternoon I was resting on the bed with a fringed coverlet over me and tucked up under my shoulders. The fringe was tickling my chin;

I started to brush the coverlet away but before I could move, it folded itself away from my chin as if some unseen hand was there, reading my thoughts and wanting to be helpful! I was very surprised but kindly thanked whoever had removed the cover. My intuition was instructing me that whoever was responsible the intention behind this act was genuine and caring. Just as the gentleman spirit who turns the garage light on and off for us is only trying to be helpful. Pranks however still seem to be intermingled with the benevolence but they are harmless, cheerful pranks laced with their humor.

My purses and belts are moved around regularly. I sometimes find a belt standing straight up in the air on the bed or stairs, and my purses are at times balanced precariously in unusual places, such as balanced on a bottom rung of a chair! And once I found an apple in our fruit bowl balanced upon a smaller piece of fruit beneath it and half into thin air! Apparently time, space, nor gravity has meaning on the other side. In this same vein I have found the chains in our grandfathers' clock *braided* like a hair braid! It was a job to straightened them back out.

More than once when I sat down at my vanity to put on my makeup the tray of items which had been quite a mess, all of a sudden was arranged in perfect order! I have invisible help!

Returning home one night we found the most beautiful and amazing drawings of Angel wings, imprinted into my bedroom carpeting! After we calmed down I was able to tip-toe to my bed, getting on top of it to take pictures. I wanted to video and take pictures of the amazing designs! We were beside ourselves at the beauty we had found of this phenomenal floor art! It had not been there an hour before! Every empty space of carpet was perfectly imprinted with the drawing of wings! We realized the Heavenly Beings can do anything! My pictures show what we see as angel wings all over the carpet in the room and each one was perfect! I had recently written a true life experience about my son and our miracle at that time for Guideposts, Angels on Earth. I took these magnificent angel drawings to point to my story! We would find more angel drawings' as more experiences carried on in our lives. By the way, the next day or so I received a letter saying my story was accepted be printed in Angels on Earth!

The old antique floor lamp that sits beside Leon's chair apparently gets in the way of our guests who regularly seem to bump into it. Several times a week we hear a bump noise, and find the lamp and lampshade swaying. I am sure it stands in one of our friendly spirits path or is for attention and no harm is ever done.

David has a large wooden oriental box on the wall filled with small antique objects. One day as I passed by this box I heard a loud noise like it was falling off of the wall I spun around quickly to catch the falling box but it had not moved!

Similarly, practically every night I hear the floorboards upstairs groaning and giving way as though the spiritual traffic is straining them. The spirits go on with doing their tasks as in their earthly lives. Can you imagine how busy they are?

One afternoon while I was cleaning out a storage trunk I took out a large box containing a collector's doll that belongs to my granddaughter. The second I had laid it down someone threw the lid off! I knew it was Katie Jane who had gotten excited about seeing the doll! I told her to look as long as she liked and I told her about the doll while I waited. It may be hard for some of you to understand that she is still just a little girl, even though she is in spirit. But as these wonderful experiences occur I understand more of how the spirits here go about their daily lives. I'm sure many of you know what I mean when I have sometimes said, "Is this a dream or is it real?" Most days I cannot simply understand how all of this can happen, but it is real and it does happen!

On several occasions when I have gone upstairs to our bedroom to get something or to clean, I have found several of my daughter's old dolls and a teddy bear that I have kept, all lined up on my bed! At times Katie has tucked them in under my blanket or bedspread! I knew for some reason Katie Jane had done this when she had been playing. I also have an old wicker doll carriage with dolls in it in my bedroom. At times it will be gone from the bedroom and all I can find are the carriage tracks, which go straight through my dresser as if it weren't there! The tracks are plainly indented in the carpets leading from where I kept the carriage to a new location that Katie Jane has chosen to push it to! Once, I found it in a closet and once on top of our kitchen bar!

During a visit a dear friend of ours pointed out Katie's tiny footprints in the carpet, I was quite surprised he took notice even though her footprints were very clear and showing up white! He was quite amazed to experience this. We live between two different worlds every day and look forward to each tomorrow. He is also the one who swore he saw a white rose tree in our yard! He kept walking around the house and just knew he had seen a rose tree!

We had been awaiting a surgical procedure needed by my daughter Lynn. The date arrived and while she was in surgery we were in the waiting room at the hospital I looked up and saw Lynn, sort of floating into the room! She floated to in front of me and said, "not to worry about her that everything would be alright and she would be just fine." She also told me what was being done to her and the procedure. I mentally replied to her that I knew she would be all right and that I loved her, and then she faded away. This happened because of being able to see her with my clairvoyance. An hour later she was out of surgery and brought to her room. The first thing she said when she opened her eyes was, "Did you know that I came to you in the waiting room and told you everything would be just fine?" I exclaimed that I did! Soon the surgeon came in to explain the procedure and to tell us of a tumor he had removed. This information I already knew about since Lynn had already told me when she floated into the waiting room.

I followed him into the hall after he had finished talking and told him of the experience that Lynn and I had shared in the waiting room. He smiled broadly and said, "If you only knew some of the stories I have heard over the years---that happens during surgery or a grave illness." I discovered later that the doctor's sister was very *psychic* so he apparently was familiar with paranormal phenomena. We thought that was great!

Years before when I was fairly new with my lessons into the paranormal world, I used to see golden lights around my mother. It was when she was in the hospital and her attending physicians didn't think she would live much longer. I told the doctor that I saw the lights and I took them to mean that my mother would be alright, at least for the time being. I didn't elaborate however, because I saw the look of disbelief in his eyes. I was only trying to reassure him, since I knew he had lost a son not too long before.

I must remember the rule to never force such information onto people who are not ready to hear it. Death is the ultimate healing you know, and I know the doctor will see his son again and his joy will be great. My mother, incidentally passed away in November of 1994, and since that time I have seen her while I have been both awake and asleep. She is always young and vibrant looking. She lets me know she is happy and sends messages of love and trust. I have especially appreciated her comforting appearances during times of stress; she seems to know just when I need her the most, such as when a loved one is ill. She gives me courage when I need it.

Another fond memory of her and my dad is when my son and I went to see her in the nursing home. The meager amount of costume jewelry that my mother owned had recently been stolen from her bedside. As a present the previous Christmas David had given her a gold panther pin along with a sweater to wear it on. Her pin was among the missing items. Mom was too sick to wear it anymore now but it meant allot to her.

As we drove home David became very quiet and all of a sudden said, "He had just received a message from my dad and mother both." David relayed the beautiful message to me and then added as a confirmation of the authenticity of the message they had told him, "we would find something made of gold from them at the house when we got home. This was something that they had arranged for us to discover." Upon arriving I went straight upstairs to change clothes. As I stepped into my bedroom I stopped dead in my tracks! The first thing I saw was something brightly shining. I stepped closer in the dusk light and there was my mothers' gold panther pin on my antique teddy bear! I immediately called for David to come and see this wonderful sign from mother and dad. This demonstrated beyond a doubt that they were still working together in our behalf, even though they were separated by death. How much more proof could one ask for?

Now, I am being compelled by the Christ like Beings of Light to write this Bible verse for the people, who are non-believers, judge others, and who live in fear...

CORINTHIANS 12:24 it clearly states;

Now about spiritual gifts, brothers, I do not want you to be ignorant. You know that when you were pagans, somehow or other you were influenced and led astray to dumb idols. Therefore I tell you that no one who is speaking by the spirit of God says,
And the same Spirit and he give them to each one, just as he determines. You that no one who is speaking by the Spirit of God says, "Jesus be cursed" and no one can say, "Jesus is Lord," except by the Holy Spirit.

There are different kinds of gifts, but the same Spirit. There are different kinds of service, but the same Lord. There are different kinds of working, but the same God works all of them in all men.

Now to each one the manifestation of the Spirit is given for the common good. To one there is given through the Spirit the message of wisdom, to another the message of knowledge, by means of the same Spirit, to another faith by the same Spirit, to another gifts of healing by that one Spirit, to another miraculous powers, to another prophecy, to another the ability to distinguish between spirits, to another the ability to speak in different kinds of tongues, and to still another the interpretation of tongues. All these are the work of one and the same Spirit and he gives them to each one, just as he determines.

CHAPTER FOUR
Angels, Protectors and Past Life Experiences

I began this book when the other side told me to start writing our story, and when I needed a break from the physical work that we all cope with every day. It has been a time of higher learning on my Spiritual path and a regeneration for me. I trust that what I have written will be of assistance to people who perhaps have not yet known of others who have experienced episodes perhaps similar to those I have experienced. The process of writing the book has not been easy and my family at times has perhaps been hard pressed to understand all of my reasons for writing it.

My husband and some of my children, despite the adventure into the paranormal that we share, have mainly known me as wife and mother, not author. But though they do not fully understand my reasons for writing they have been encouraging nevertheless. But write I must, as I have been urged to do from the Christ Light Beings, I have lived through it long enough and I have been told to share the experiences, so now it's time to put it down on paper.

Already, because of my writing our oldest daughter has begun to speak more freely of her own contact with the paranormal. She recently said, "That she has seen herself in what appeared to her to be a former life many years ago and that I came to her while she was dreaming, telling her she had once been named Robin Harrison sometime in the early nineteenth century." She related to me that in this vision state I had taken her to a cemetery where she had been buried under a lot of beautiful trees and that she could see herself as she was then, and as she is in this time now. We spoke of many things during this special time together. Perhaps, one day we will come upon this cemetery and be able to place flowers upon the gravestone of Robin Harrison. I found this experience to be very beautiful by sharing it together and I intuitively feel sure I know where this cemetery is…

I have seen myself in further lifetimes as well and during periods of three different wars where I have been both male and female, different cultures, and from other countries many times. Egypt and Germany are two wartime locations and India is the third. I seem to be rescuing young victims, the children of war and taking them to safety. I was a warrior again in those times and the same as in India. I also have seen myself as a very poor but contented woman. I have lived as male and female, all colors and cultures…

In one time period I was a member of a harem a dancer wrapped in veils! I've always thought it was strange how we are for no apparent reason attracted to this and that in our current lifetimes. I believe we have some unconscious memory of our previous existences and are drawn to similar things now. It may be certain foods, cultures, sports, hobbies, the work we want to do, talents of music, arts, and so on which we find attracted too. And also the people who we are drawn too.

How many people do what we think are impossible? Even small children who can play a concerto on the piano without a lesson? There are some who are handicapped in one or another, but are brilliant in some other extraordinary way. Occurrences like these that seem impossible to us. Where do you think this talent and knowing comes from?

For instance, that is seeing myself as a dancer in past lives and now once more drawn to dancing, learning without lessons and able to choreograph dance routines for competition. I found this easy to do and I have had no formal training in dance. I performed for years at various kinds of auditions, functions, shows and events. Dancing has always seemed to come easy for me, perhaps my years in the harem linger somehow and have aided me in this regard. Who knows?

As I have mentioned above my spiritual growth has been accompanied by a much clearer spiritual vision. That is, my ability to see spiritual forms seems to be increasing all the while. I have also learned to trust my intuition much more, and it always proves itself to be trustworthy.

For instance, I recall a young couple sitting beside David and myself in a restaurant. The man was so proud and attentive to the young blond woman that he was with I marveled at how good he was to her and I admired that, even though her face had been burnt extensively. I could only see the love in his eyes for her. I mentioned this to David when we left the restaurant. He looked shocked as he replied, "there was nothing wrong with her face she was beautiful!" We both instantly knew I was shown either a past life, or a future tragedy to come. Those times are hard to separate, to bow and go on knowing I was shown this for a reason in my teachings. I do not question why I am shown different things I just trust and realize it's for a very important reason.

One of the things that make me feel restless is when I receive a message from the other side and fail, due to the prospect of embarrassment to pass it along to the person for whom it was intended. This was also a large part of my lessons and in time I would be given the reasoning. So, in other words, you take everything you are given and view it as positive. Needless to say I am writing this book in relative secrecy, only confiding in very few who are true believers which is my family.

Usually, however, when I have risked relaying messages to strangers or to individuals whom I know will not understand I can trust that whether or not they seem to appreciate the words at the time, some will come to appreciate them later if only in secret. When they have spoken to me later to my delight, they have expressed that the messages were of great comfort and very accurate.

In a reading for someone I never know what information will be given to me or my son for that person, but we do know it's what they are to have from the other side. We cannot special order any information for anyone, no one can. We can ask questions for a person and sometimes the specific words they need to hear come through. It comes as it should and for what they can handle and if the timing is right for that answer. I believe we need to learn to trust and learn and that is called faith.

If we knew all the answers in life why would we need to come to this earth school? I have been told by the Beings of Light there are many lessons and experiences each of us are here to learn in life. They cannot supply all of the answers they must step back from us for our lesson. They are with us to help guide us but they cannot fix everything. I have at times asked, "If they can do an intervention?" and I have seen this happen, I call this a miracle.

It is my belief, and it is redundant to say, that we visualize heaven as we were taught it to be. Our picture of heaven in other words is conditioned by our religious beliefs and cultural environment. And again, however we imagine it to be and however it actually is, I am convinced that it may be compared to a recess of sorts, during which we recharge, debrief, and rest. Perhaps during our heavenly recess we may spend some time as a guardian angel for someone else, on earth. That is, if we choose to do so --- free will remember --- until or if we choose to reincarnate in order to evolve to a higher level of consciousness. Evolving to a higher level of consciousness for me can be summarized easily, as we learn to love ourselves regardless for who we are, we grow toward heaven right here on earth. And because of my positive friendly spirits and guardian angels I have learned that I am not only my Heavenly Fathers creation, but also a kind of pinch off of Him. This is part of the Big Picture an indispensable part with all of my flaws notwithstanding and all is meant to be and everything will be alright in the end, regardless of the heartache along the way. Everything will be how it was designed to be in the beginning. My spirits and guardians, my son and the heavenly beings have taught me that, and I thank the Heavenly Father for sending them to me every day. They have all worked hard to gain my attention and have continued teaching me every day. My son knew all of this would happen as my teacher. So much he waited for me to recall from our other lives.

I recall the day I mentally received the following message: When you can't see the forest for the trees. That evening I happened across the same thought in a book that I was reading. I knew the message must have great meaning for me since I had been exposed to it twice in the same day. I had been wrestling within myself regarding some friends who had been critical of my new experiences both to my face and behind my back. I felt sad and hurt because of how much I do love them, and have supported them in the past. I took this duplicate message to mean that it would be best if I bowed (meaning walk away) before them and then detached myself from them and their negativity. In realizing one must leave others behind on their own path as we open ourselves up to higher planes of existence. There will be some drawn to us but others, as I have learned, will become afraid, indignant, and just generally condemning.

One of the latest condemning words to me came from someone I have known a long time and love. As I spoke of my experiences that another friend was interested in, this other friend became very angry, accusing me of worshiping spirits! I was taken by surprise and the hurt inflicted was so great I did not respond. My interested other friend who had asked the questions was shocked at our friend and of her behavior. After a while of silence others began to try to start another conversation directed away from all of this.

The next few weeks I pondered over the event and realized again how I was warned ahead of time with the quote in the book and leaving those behind. Yes, little by little I was learning many important things. My spiritual teachers know when and how to direct my messages ahead in many different ways to help me in my work. One important thing I have been taught well is to always HOLD my ground with my heavenly teachings.

Recently, something new began to occur in the family room during the evenings. As I sat down one night to relax, many images and letters began to float across the white closet door! I thought what now! Some of the images were of hearts and profiles of men and women's faces. There appeared next, all kinds of symbols and shadow people. Some of the letters appeared to be in oriental script, perhaps Chinese. I kept exclaiming to my husband, "Can you see it? Can you see it?" Over and over he replied, "No, I can't." Leon was used to hearing me tell about the faces in our magic mirror, and now I apparently had a *whiteboard* to watch every evening.

At times I could detect a note of sarcasm in his voice when he said, "What's on it now?" He probably wondered how much longer all of this would go on! He would continue to watch television and I would sit, pen and paper in hand, in case any clear messages were forthcoming and watch my whiteboard. Appearing in the drawings were different animals and even our ghostly lumberjack at times. I especially enjoyed the gold and blue sparkles, soft in texture that would sometimes float toward me looking like bubbles from this closet door. I told Leon what I was watching was a thousand times better than any television program! This lesson went on for several weeks and I wrote down as many of the letters, symbols, people, animals, and so on that I could. I felt this had a lot to do with the signs under which we are born (horoscopes) that I had been learning about for some time. I knew one thing for sure this was very important and whatever the reason when the time was right for me, I would know, and I found out I was right. Every direction they pointed me too I was learning!

In September I really had to restrain myself from shouting to Leon, "Can you see them?" I was still painting on the house and I sat down on a paint can during a break, wondering if we were ever going to finish painting the exterior of our house. As I looked up admiring the beauty of the trees I saw what looked like bicycle chains or links, situated between the trees and me! These tiny objects were floating throughout the entire yard and everywhere I looked! I sat in awe of this seemingly never-ending event in amazement! It looked as if it was snowing! My sight had changed to a new and wonderful way. This would be another gift to help me. This was amazing my new sight was multidimensional...Wow!

Beverly told me later, "I was seeing into a realm that few people could experience." From that day on I see these tiny little links floating everywhere in the air. When I ride in our car with Leon I gaze incessantly at them---I see them as molecules, eons and energy forms that one needs a high powered microscope in order to see them. They are inside and outside; I see them wherever I go. I know it's not an eye problem as I have had my eyes checked and once more, I can see these energies at *will* anytime. They seem to be in some kind of pattern which dissolves into everything. I have no trouble in seeing so many things that were not *visible* to me before. It is such a *mystical* and *magical* world we live in. This is what the angels have taught and told me about. They have told me to always remember: "To enjoy every day, to love life, embrace life, and that life is the greatest gift we can ever receive here on earth, and to learn from it." I am so happy that I have been shown to me how all of us have such a loving and forgiving Universal Father, not one to fear. Our Universal Father is all about love and compassion; straight from the heart and that's what matters. This is what I have been taught.

One day sitting in a coffee shop I had one of my premonitions. I unexpectedly saw an airplane take off out of New York, a TWA jetliner, and as it flew off the runway it burst into flames! The great part of this was I saw everyone on board get out ok. That evening when I came home and was watching the late news, the same scary event was announced: A TWA plane had caught fire just after take-off, just as I had witnessed earlier that morning and in that location. There were no injuries, thank goodness!

My son and I get many of these things from time to time. We feel helpless even when knowing it is for a reason. No one can change destiny except the Creator! We carry a lot of weight on us being as we both are and that we cannot speak of. Family is the hardest to know about before any tragedy. Our work is not without great sorrow at times.

Later in the fall of that same year my son had a most marvelous experience by way of what was almost a terrible tragedy. Around 1:30 pm in the afternoon I suddenly became very ill and had to lie down my legs would not hold me up and I felt very strange! In about 30 minutes I began to sense an urgency that I needed to call David in the state where he lived. I told his dad that we needed to go to him at once! I knew something was terribly wrong with him and I became very weak and disoriented in the driveway nearly fainting.

Inside the house I had to lie down. Suddenly we received a telephone call from a hospital in the city where my son lived. His neighbor Jane was at this hospital where my son had been taken! She was calm but telling us to COME now! Then I knew why I felt the distress I had! We drove as fast as possible to get to him. On the way I asked for a sign that he would live, a large cross in the sky. It wasn't long and there it was! It stayed with us for miles and I knew he would be ok. I still couldn't get there fast enough! His dad and I were really worried and had not been told about his heart failing. We only knew he had double pneumonia.

David had been found in his neighbors' yard where he had collapsed from double pneumonia! His neighbor friend quickly drove him to the hospital where he was brought in D.O.A. (dead on arrival.) He had died in the man's car on the way! He had had a heart attack and drown in his own fluid! After working on him for some time the doctor never gave up, and he was somehow able to revive him. David was dead for such a long time the heart specialist told me, "He couldn't believe that my son had come back to life, that he shouldn't be here and he was still in bad shape and not near out of the woods yet."

This wonderful doctor never gave up on David thank God...I went into his room and I did not recognize him! He was connected to all kind of medical machines and tubes. He had lost so much weight his face was sunken in. David immediately sensed I was there and opened his eyes some, and even tried to manage a little smile. He was so happy to see me as I was him! I held his hand as I sat close to him and told him, "I would be right here beside him and to rest."

89

My son told me, "When he died he left his body and entered a tunnel of lights, whereupon he called out to Beverly for help!"According to my son he could see the spirit of Beverly; she had appeared to him, with him, in the tunnel. He told her, "He wanted to stay in the wonderful, loving lights but knew, somehow, that it was not time to do so. His strong love for me, his family, and his sense of tasks yet to be accomplished was impelling him back. He remembered Beverly then assisted him back."

The next thing he remembers was being back in his body and in his hospital bed, looking for his father and me, and he weakly tried to call out for us. By then some time had passed and at that moment he gazed over to his left and saw Katie Jane, our spirit child sitting at his bedside. She had her big toothless smile from ear to ear, swinging her little legs back and forth. He tried to smile when he saw her radiant face she was all bubbly and happy, just like any child might look full of love for a loved one. As weak as he was he slightly moved his hand to her and she put her tiny hand in his. Katie radiated absolute healing and love to him, and in him. Her happy presence and her over-whelming love, healing, and compassion was sent straight to his heart and soul, a moment he would carry with him forever. She stayed close by him the entire time he was hospitalized. She calls him "her brother," so I am positive in another time, or perhaps many times they have been siblings.

While he was still critical with his heart he had a second leaving of his body in a NDE. He remembered clearly he began to see another form take shape at the end of his bed. This was the form of a Catholic nun, dressed in the old style of full habit of blue and white, and glowing in golden light. She had a blue cross on the head piece, a nun from long ago a French nun. For a brief moment he seemed to recognize her and could hear her thoughts to him behind her continual smile. She told him, "he would be healed" and then she opened out her arms to him as if to embrace him with her total love. She appeared to be floating slightly above the floor with her garments softly flowing about her. She passed healing to him with Christ's love then faded from the room. I realized later that I had become ill at the very moment my son had collapsed and died with pneumonia and a heart attack by drowning in his fluid.

We had such a close connection I had felt his pain, and when I spoke with Beverly later, she also knew something had happened to him and suddenly could think of nothing else but David. I was slowly beginning to realize that some of us help others in many ways that cannot be explained. I was to be enlightened on these things as time went by and into my work of spiritual healing with my son. Somehow, I knew we would work as a team throughout our lives once again. Most of his life he suffered silently with his illness but he never left his mission, it was helping all of the people he could.

One night, during sleep I had a most marvelous experience and lesson. I was taken in a vision state to a beautiful cathedral. Its pews were filled with people, and an alb-clad priest who gave off an aura of a spiritual being of light was standing up front. A woman came down a side isle to me and told me to come with her. I quickly knew to do this and together we walked down the side isle of the sanctuary adjacent to the worshipers or others who also appeared to be there for a learning experience.

She led me into a tiny room off to the side where another woman was waiting. Both of the two women had a very holy presence about them. One of the women held out a small box toward me and asked me, "to pick out a color." I didn't quite know what she meant, but upon looking into the box I saw small pieces of tapestry cloth in red and orange hues. I really didn't like any of the colors and somehow knew they were *not* right for me but choose a red piece, I didn't know what else to do. The woman holding the box smiled sweetly and said, "Choose again." when I looked in the box again I noticed that the colors and objects had changed and I choose a small piece of fabric that I knew had the right colors for me from the box.

Then I noticed I was standing upon some kind of doctors scales as if to be weighed. The woman then said, "Too smell the fabric I had chosen." As I did, I suddenly vanished from the scene at an incredible speed up through the air! I had absolutely no weight to me as I flew, and the feeling was well, I do not have words to describe the freedom and complete happiness I felt from earthly ties! I was free to go anyplace faster than thought! I was a part of everything and all there is.

I knew this lesson indicated how it feels to actually leave one's body at the time of physical death. When I returned back to the small room I was standing upon the scales once more. I knew without a doubt this *valuable* lesson did indicate how when we each leave here to return home, the physical body is shed. This heavy outer layer around us we carry and then at death we are entirely free in every sense. How wonderful to have this experience confirming what I am being taught by the heavenly beings of light! I will never forget this amazing lesson! Since that experience I can say with complete authenticity, that I do not fear death at all and what a simple transition death is. As one of my spiritual teachers has said, "it's only a breath away the veil is so very thin, between here and there." This was amazing to experience! I would be using this information for others one day.

I keep a dream logbook of all my experiences and eagerly look forward to my nightly lessons every night from the other side, and eagerly look forward to each one!

One wonderful experience happened on February 13, 1993, the date of my dad's birthday --- My son and I went to hear the music of a Native American Indian play his flute at a concert in a nearby city. His name is Jesse and he is from Arizona. The music was beautiful, enchanting, almost haunting, it moved me and many others to tears several times. After the concert David and I went to meet Jesse to tell him how much his music moved us. Jesse looked at David and held out one of his tapes to him and said, "I have been waiting for you, I have two tapes left and will not make more of this music, you are to have this one and give the other one to Beverly." We were shocked and delighted, and with the surprise tape for Beverly. Neither of us had ever met Jesse before nor had Beverly. How did he know her name? Only he knows that. The tape has been a treasure to us since and we were fortunate enough to meet Jesse another two times. We three became the best of friends on our journeys.

Upon returning home that same evening Leon who has a severe hearing loss was sleeping in the car all the way home. Later, he began to talk about listening to Jesses tape on the way home in the car! He had been sitting in the back seat. "But you couldn't have heard the music from the tape, the tape player is broken we could not play it!" He looked as shocked as the two of us! All I know is that he heard Jesse's music all the way home! I could still hear his magical flute music in my head that night. I sat up wide awake that night and I began to see many designs, and seas of energies floating in the room where I was.

I was sitting in the bedroom and later I was still too exhilarated to sleep. At that point I began to see all sizes of hearts floating in the room ceiling to floor, which I knew to be Valentine symbols from my dad, he

92

was sending not only Valentine greetings but it was also his birthday! All of a sudden my father's spirit form emerged floating out from the direction of the magic mirror. He appeared as a translucent golden shape with a brilliant circle of cobalt blue in the center of his forehead where the *third* eye resides.

He sort of floated over to in front of me and I thanked him for coming! I was so happy and told him how very much he is loved and missed here, and my complete appreciation for all his years of devotion to me. By then I was near tears from the beauty and intimacy of these special moments. I mentally asked him if he could show me himself as he appeared in younger earthly life and he did so, appearing young, healthy, and happy. He looked so young, and in his prime, as he once was here on earth. Oh, how I wanted everyone to be able to share these wonderful experiences, to let them know our loved ones are still so alive! And, I still believe Jesse had something to do with this anniversary encounter.

It was soon summer, when one of our beloved spirits saved my life! Leon was working one day on the old exterior siding and in the process had opened a small hole in the side of the house. He then went on to work for a couple of weeks on another area on a different side of our home thinking nothing of it.

I awoke one day and as I lay there thinking of chores that I had to get accomplished I saw my main teacher float out of the magic mirror! It was Han Tai Chen Su; he was life- sized and rather solid looking! I was mesmerized watching as he traveled (floating) across the top of the stairway and dissolved into my closet wall! "What is he doing?" I asked myself. I waited a few minutes and when I didn't see him return into view I got up and went towards the closet. Before I got there however, I heard a loud *roaring* noise! Looking over at the stairs I noticed that there were hundreds of bees there and in part of the bedroom, on the stairway, the hall area, the curtains, carpets, and all over the furniture! I thought I was watching a horror movie! I couldn't comprehend this!

I immediately ran the opposite direction away from the bees slamming the bedroom doors behind me as I ran! I ran down the back stairway to the garage to get the bee spray, then returning into the house I crept back in. As I opened the double doors to the front parlor the bees were everywhere! I knew I had to do something quickly, and although I had no shoes on and wearing just a summer pair of pajamas I walked right through the swarms of bees into the parlor! I could see a tiny opening up on the stair landing ceiling. It was there in and out of, which the bees were moving! My only focus was to stop the bees. I climbed on a chair that was in the parlor and sprayed into the small hole they were coming out of and then taped it shut fast!

What a noise then! I got out of there running, shutting the doors behind me as I went. I carefully made my way back upstairs on the back stairs to our bedroom. I quickly noticed that there were no bees around the bed even though they were thick everywhere else, as if there were some sort of invisible line drawn across the room past the foot of the bed! I immediately knew why my teacher had let me see him he had protected me! The hole into which I had sprayed was right under the closet where my teacher had traveled trying to show me the nest was there! He was warning me, showing me the location of the danger! The bees had sat up a nest between the ceilings from the small hole left by Leon from the exterior. This was a *nightmare*! I could have been stung to death! I felt my life had been saved by my teacher!

I called our regional poison control center and they responded quickly since some of the spray had hit me in the face. The woman who answered my call had me call her throughout the day to tell her I was all right. She said, "This call also reminded her of a *horror* movie!" Leon is highly allergic to bee stings and did not notice the bees early it may have been because it was dark yet when he dressed quickly and left. I just know later on he said, "He did not see the bees, since he usually went into our bathroom to get ready for work so the lights wouldn't disturb me." Who knows? But because of my spiritual warning we were both able to escape being stung, maybe even to death by hundreds of bees! How grateful we are to this spiritual being that protected us on that day, especially with Leon being so allergic to bees. I felt as if my spiritual teacher had defiantly saved our lives!

Later in the fall of that year I began to study the Runes; I knew this was another lesson in order to teach me more focus, to assist myself in particularly difficult situations. The Rune stones helped to quiet my mind and open myself to new possibilities that otherwise may not have been presented to me. Between the Runes, listening to my dreams, out of body astral traveling, and my ever expanding second sight and intuition, I am often able to see through the superficial part of a person's behavior or comments. I then can perceive a deeper, more central reason for the activity. Many times these gifts warn me of malevolence, jealousy, or outright scornful people with a negative intent.

My soon to come even newer vision showed me this lesson in another way. In the vision I was holding a box of snakes, putting my hand into the box because I trusted, but many of which bit me! Then later, the next day, a friend called me and displayed quite a bit of *hostility* toward me, attacking me on account of my spiritual journey. Though I did not know exactly what the snakebite vision meant at the time I was instinctively put on guard because of it. I was more ready when the hostile person called and I was somewhat prepared. I knew the vision was a warning to be very careful.

Though this particular dream about snakes seems to have been a premonition of aggression, I have also begun to take notice of symbols of snakes. Particularly the Caduceus image of twin snakes around a staff or the single-snake image around the staff of Aesculapius, the old Roman god of medicine. Both adopted by the medical professions that seem to be associated with an impending, and at least potential, healing ministry I would be working in soon.

One day after I had been thinking about the healing symbols I happened to sit down on my bed a moment. Suddenly, a beautiful clear voice called out to me, "what does thou seek most?" Without hesitation at all I called out, "to help others!" I knew with all my heart that this was a Christ light Heavenly Being! There are no words in our language to describe the feelings' that ran through me! I was completely humbled and in awe of what had just occurred. This was one of the greatest changes in my life! Not knowing how this would take place I only knew it would. I was told the next day by the other side "I would be working in a healing ministry." I would continue to hear out loud many heavenly messages guiding me, and experience much more from then on. I was just beginning!

A few days later I was drawn to go to in front of the magic mirror. To my surprise I felt compelled to even go closer. To my astonishment I was mentally told, "To hold out my hands, palms upward." I then witnessed shades of emerald green light flowing out of my eyes, nose, mouth, throat, the palms of my hands, and the center of my heart! At that moment I was given the words once more, "I would at some point in the near future be engaged in a healing ministry!"

I had been reading Hands of Light, a book by Barbara Ann Brennan, which speaks of various kinds of energies and alternative healing techniques that are available to us. I took my experience to confirm that I too, would be learning even more about these energies in order to utilize them for the purpose of healing. Yes, everything is connected as I was being told. We are all connected and a part of all there is! I had known in my heart this was all true. I never questioned how this would happen I only knew it would, I believed. I had faith and trusted completely.

In connection with this experience by accident, I soon heard of a person who already had such a ministry; she is a relative of a friend of mine. One day while visiting by phone with my friend I told her about my healing experience and she replied, "her relative who lives many miles away worked in some kind of healing." I was elated! This would be my first baby steps along my new found path the door had opened for me! A person who would be able to assist me on my journey. Through my friend I contacted this person in the next few days asking her about her work, and inquiring about whether she would favor me with a meeting. She was very kind, consented to the meeting and even invited me to stay in her home since I would be traveling some distance in order to see her. Her Reiki Master teacher was coming to teach as he did yearly. He would take me into his classes. I had trusted with all my heart and now I was being led with everything falling into place. Before I left home I asked for a sign from my Heavenly Universal Father to make clear to me whether or not I was on the right track. I wanted a confirmation that I was taking the right steps in my work.

A short time later I was outside in the back yard with my two small granddaughters enjoying our day together. It was an extremely dry season without rain for many days. All of a sudden one of my little granddaughters looked up into the sky and said, "Look ma-ma an upside down *rainbow*!" I was spellbound as I took in this beautiful extraordinary sight realizing this was my confirmation from my Heavenly Father! I had trusted with all my heart and believed in the promise, the way, and here it was! It was the *rainbow* for which this book and the introductory poem are named. A half circle with its ends pointing upward toward the heavens not downward towards the earth in all seven beautiful colors in all its glory! I ran for my camera and as soon as I had taken several pictures it disappeared from sight just like that! This experience truly changed my life.

When the pictures were developed not only was the upside down *rainbow* plainly visible, but when one turns the picture sideways a ministering angel is clearly seen there! An Angel form, which I have firmly embraced as my confirmation. Not only of the love that fills the universe but of the compassionate, teaching ministry into which I have been for some reason drawn. I feel the only ones to see this extraordinary event was the three of us and for our eyes only. The *rainbow* disappeared as soon as I took my pictures! From this day forward I would be on my life mission in a very exciting, wonderful way, and I felt like shouting it to the world!

I feel that much of one's time is spent questioning what our mission is about and why are we here. Now that I had a good idea of mine I felt good knowing I should be able to help others now. All of the loving spiritual beings around me have changed my outlook on life completely and I am grateful. They have helped to lead me to this stage in my life and without them, well, I wonder where would I be by now? I would not trade or change anything that has happened to me for anything knowing I have evolved to new and higher levels of new lessons and learning. Yes, life with all of the hardships is beautiful and wonderful in my new world of spiritual teachers and guides.

One of my new lessons given to me one evening came from a beautiful angel being and gave me much to think about. The angels words seemed so simple and possible to accomplish. This was in one of my hard times of decision when the angel appeared and stated, "One has the choice in life to create a thorn garden or a flower garden. Each day one has their own choice that make." I hope to always remember to use my own free will to choose and design my days.

CONCLUSION

I began my healing ministry by applying my new energies toward my family with surprising if not dramatic results. And while I was with my newly acquainted friend who was in this healing ministry, I too, was healed of an ongoing health problem I had for many years. I have not had this problem since this whole experience began and I am so thankful for this. Perhaps a benevolent, intentional and therapeutic touch, coupled with enthusiasm and knowledge, as well as one's spiritual belief, are all that is necessary to work wonders. I do know I am a true believer in the heavenly beings who are showing us the way, and my son who is a spiritual teacher and healer combined with our spiritual work here on earth. We both are more than honored to be passing Christ's love and energy coming from our Universal Father. Everything we both do to help others is through this highest power and the high Council.

I continue to work in the capacity of a medium and Reiki Master teacher/ practitioner to stay attuned to messages intended for my own continued growth as well as for the growth of others. In this regard beginning soon I was taught about automatic writing. I first clear my mind and write the words I am given, basically without thinking. Automatic writing is not a necessary tool in order to receive messages, but is a valuable tool in relaxing the mind, releasing all material concerns, learning, and a generally restful state as well. The new information I receive is astounding to me sometimes covering serious everyday concerns, universal lessons, ancient information, and answers in my work.

There is a reason for everything I am being taught and I realize this, and as far as readings go, I receive them in various ways as you see. The connection to the departed, the other side, is always an instant one for me. It does not matter where I am or what I may be doing. Automatic writing for me is sometimes pages of information so I write it all down because I could not possibly remember it all. Many times I will be told to sit down and write information right then. What I receive may also be on world events, crop-circles, Aliens, or any subject, or for any person. I never know what I will get.

My Mothers passing

When my mother approached her passing, during her final hospitalization I was able to draw on my new found strength, and release her into the arms of the Heavenly Father, the Universe and my dad. She had waited and suffered being a prisoner in her body and now it was her time. Nineteen years to me was more than enough for her to suffer. I was with her that last day at the hospital; when suddenly I could see her life force energy floating out of the top of her head at the crown area. I knew this meant her body was shutting down and it would not be long until she left here, her aura was breaking up. Then I was told to go home by the Being of Light to rest for a short while.

Later, at home I heard a heavenly voice tell me, "it was time to go back and tell my mother once more anything I needed yet to tell her." I was able to be with her shortly before she passed over and even though she was in a coma like state I knew she could hear me. I spoke words of love to her knowing she wanted to be reunited with dad. I then released her into the arms of my dad and I know she will never be alone and in fact has never been alone. I was told once more by my spiritual beings to go home I would be called soon. I did not want to leave mom but obeyed, I knew they were right. Her soul was long gone now out of her body. I knew no one ever dies alone there are passed over loved ones and heavenly beings waiting to help each soul on just as my dad came to get my mother.

My spiritual friends you see have taught me that we are never alone now or on the other side. We are it seems by definition surrounded in this life by all sorts of spiritual companions, ghosts, spirits, conscious beings, guides, teachers, beneficent lights, deceased loved ones, and an overarching Presence of love in which we all live and move and have our being. Quite a picture, uh? It's the Big Picture and because of my spirits no longer do I embrace my old traditional notions filled with doubt and fear. I now firmly believe that when we leave this plane of existence we continue, we go on and on, always being provided opportunities to evolve further to learn more and to become more at-one with it all. We often are tempted to think of life as only a time of suffering, perhaps sprinkled with joy and bliss to be followed by the real heaven in which all our tears will be completely and permanently wiped away. My heavenly spirits however, have caused me to question this traditional notion. I even wonder if, after we leave this life some of us do stand in line to get back here. I understand this now through my teachers and my lessons and that some things are not always as we think, and as they seem and how we have been taught growing up.

Finally, in my heart I hold the greatest love given to me by all of my Christ-like companions and it has been my son David, my spiritual family, teachers, guides, angels, and the Christ like Beings of Light, who have especially inspired the conclusion to this small book. Now that my eyes have been opened to a small part of a vast universe, I firmly believe that if we so choose we may return here to this earth plane to repeat our lives, over and over if we wish. In order to learn additional lessons that will assist us in discovering what we and it are all about. Some of us may perhaps be anxious to return to this material existence, while others may linger a bit on the other side in order to provide assistance to those who are here. Others may choose never to return, who knows for sure? But perhaps we all have our jobs to do, and as one of my own angel messengers said to me.

"Blessed are those who open their hearts to the beauty of it all. We are all a part of this great mystery called life, and life is all about sharing the love that arises from within."

I have thought long and hard on these words and as a result of this message, and as a result of all my experiences in the several years, I have concluded, that it is probably only here on earth that we can learn that there is, in fact nothing to fear, but fear itself, as I have always believed.

My next book will explain more of why the other side was preparing my son and I in so many areas. My ghosts you see gained my attention and all the rest followed. This was one of their earthly missions and they have done it well. One thing for sure is to remember our universal family will never let us down no matter what we think, they are always with us loving and assisting us all they are permitted to. Each one of us is a unique part of the whole and loved beyond anything one can imagine.

100

Our Universal Father loves us so much that he gave his only son for us, and life is the greatest gift we will ever receive. Remember this, when life seems so hard, it is in our hard times we grow more spiritually and closer to our real home, our Universal home. I can still hear the words given to me so long ago,

"leave the old ways behind now, I will show you the way, for I am the light," and this was only the beginning I never looked back."

My story doesn't end here it was only our beginning and our experiences have become even much greater. Many more precious experiences and "miracles" continue on that I will write about in my next book with unheard of amazing lessons that we are still living…

I strongly feel each person who reads this book is compelled too in some way and for reasons of their own.

My next book The Story of David is to be released in December of 2014.

Web Site
WWW.Universal conversations.com

Author

Ruth Ann Friend

About the Author

Ruth Ann Friend

An ordinary housewife and the mother of four children, has learned through her own personal experiences based on her psychic gifts and abilities that she was given to communicate with the spirits of men, women, and children, who have passed onto the other side. The author has the rare ability to bridge the gap between the physical and the spiritual worlds, providing comfort to those who have lost loved ones. She then brings back powerful messages from the other side providing comfort, that life goes on in spirit and that we are eternal. She explains that on the other side we continue to choose with the free will we have all been given and we have only shed our physical body, that we needed while existing on earth.

Growing up she was not aware of her special abilities. It was only after she came to terms with who she was after a Near Death Experience. Being D.O.A. (dead on arrival) she became able to translate the souls messages into an ability to help others.

Ruth Ann lives in a small Midwestern town and works in a healing ministry. She teaches whoever is eager to learn the true meaning of unconditional love and free will. She is also a psychic reader by being connected to the other side passing messages from their world back to loved ones here. Ruth Ann also gives workshops on the paranormal, hypnosis, reincarnation/ past lives, Heavenly Beings and other worlds.

This story is only the beginning with other books forth coming in the near future that will tell more phenomenal true stories and other extraordinary events that continue on with the author and her son David.

Both of them has persevered together from their beginning, working in other spiritual realms with Archangels, passed over souls and Christ Light Beings. You will be absolutely astounded with the knowledge and universal travels they have been blessed to experience in order to tell others. This book has been written as a large part of their dedicated promise to the Creator tin order to pass along their untold story.

www.ingramcontent.com/pod-product-compliance
Lightning Source LLC
Chambersburg PA
CBHW060546100426

42742CB00013B/2477